Sentence Composing
for College

Sentence Composing for College

A **Worktext on Sentence Variety and Maturity**

Don Killgallon

Boynton/Cook Publishers
Heinemann
Portsmouth, NH

Boynton/Cook Publishers, Inc.
A subsidiary of Reed Elsevier Inc.
361 Hanover Street
Portsmouth, NH 03801–3912

Offices and agents throughout the world

Library of Congress Cataloging-in-Publication Data
Killgallon, Don.
    Sentence composing for college : a worktext on sentence variety
and maturity / Donald Killgallon.
        p.   cm.
    Includes bibliographical references.
    ISBN 0-86709-447-8
    1. English language—Sentences—Problems, exercises, etc.
2. English language—Rhetoric—Problems, exercises, etc.   I. Title
PE1441.K52   1998
808'.042—dc21   97-39392
                                                    CIP

Editor: Peter R. Stillman
Production: Elizabeth Valway
Cover design: Jenny Jensen Greenleaf
Manufacturing: Courtney Ordway

Printed in the United States of America on acid-free paper
09 08 07 06   VP   11 12 13 14

In memory of Francis Christensen, the first to see the light:

The sentence composing approach to writing improvement evolved in part from the work of the pioneering linguist Francis Christensen, who wrote in his *Notes Toward a New Rhetoric*:

> If the new grammar is to be brought to bear on composition, it must be brought to bear on the rhetoric of the sentence. . . . With hundreds of handbooks and rhetorics to draw from I have never been able to work out a program for teaching the sentence as I find it in the work of contemporary writers.

Christensen's life's work inspired this series of worktexts on sentence composing for middle school, high school, and college. I hope he would see it as "a program for teaching the sentence as [it is found] in the work of contemporary writers."

Don Killgallon

Contents

Preface   ix

Introduction   xi

1   Practicing Sentence-Composing Techniques   1

Focus 1: Sentence Unscrambling   2
Focus 2: Sentence Imitating   11
Focus 3: Sentence Combining   22
Focus 4: Sentence Expanding   36
Focus 5: Reviewing the Techniques   42

2   Using Professional Structures   49

Focus 6: Absolute Phrase   50
Focus 7: Appositive Phrase   65
Focus 8: Participial Phrase   80
Focus 9: Reviewing the Structures   97

3   Varying Professional Positions   105

Focus 10 : Sentence Openers   106
Focus 11: Subject-Verb Splits   120
Focus 12: Sentence Closers   134
Focus 13: Reviewing the Positions   148

References   157

*P*reface

When it comes to language, nothing is more satisfying than to
write a good sentence.

—*Barbara Tuchman*

This series—*Sentence Composing for Middle School*, *Sentence
Composing for High School*, and *Sentence Composing for
College*—emphasizes the most neglected unit of written
composition: the sentence. Using four sentence-manipulating
techniques—*sentence unscrambling*, *sentence imitating*,
sentence combining, and *sentence expanding*—these books
teach students structures they seldom use in their writing, but
should, and can easily use once they become familiar with them
through many examples and practices.

Each book concentrates on such structures, by means of
model sentences by professional writers. The rationale is based
on the widely accepted mimetic theory of *oral* language
acquisition, applied here to *written* language acquisition, in the
belief that continual exposure to structures used often by
professionals in their sentences will produce attention to,
understanding of, and, with practice, normal use of such
structures by students in their sentences.

The books are exercises in applied grammar, with the theory
and terminology of grammar subordinate to the major goal:
composing sentences. The naming of parts and the parsing of
sentences, the goals of traditional grammar study, are exercises
in dissection. The practices in *Sentence Composing* are exercises
in production.

The sentence-manipulating techniques are easily learned. The
practices based on them are interesting and challenging, and
they can be done by any student. In addition, the teacher can
readily give attention to the sentences students compose, with
quicker, more constant, and more thorough feedback than with
longer compositions.

Since the practices have proved successful for the great majority of students who have used them in all kinds of schools, it is demonstrably true that *Sentence Composing* can work anywhere, in any school, with any student.

Don Killgallon
Baltimore, Maryland

Introduction
How Sentence Composing Works

When you or a professional write, you both choose words and arrange them in sentences, but often with very different results: variety and maturity in sentences written by professional writers are much more evident than in sentences written by students. Unlike professional writers, students tend to write sentences similar to sentences they speak.

The big difference in variety and maturity is what this worktext is all about. The idea of sentence composing is to bridge that gap, so that your sentences more closely resemble in structure those written by professional writers. Throughout the worktext, you will see how professional writers write their sentences. You will learn and practice writing similar sentences by using four easy-to-learn techniques: *sentence unscrambling*, *sentence imitating*, *sentence combining*, and *sentence expanding*.

You will learn by imitating the pros. Just as you used imitation as a child to learn to speak by imitating experienced speakers like your parents, you can learn to write better sentences by imitating how professional writers use written language.

Nothing in the worktext is difficult to learn. You don't have to know a lot about grammar. You don't have to learn lots of terms. You don't have to study to take tests. But you do have to want to improve the sentences you write. This worktext will show you how.

First you have to learn something, and then you can go out and do it.

Mies van der Rohe

How to Use This Worktext

All practices in this worktext use model sentences written by professional writers. Throughout the worktext you will practice sentence unscrambling, sentence imitating, sentence combining, and sentence expanding to learn to write sentences that have the kind of variety and maturity in the model sentences.

You can learn a lot about writing in general through the practices in this worktext, not just about how professionals write their sentences. Even though you will be working with sentences—the backbone of all writing—you can learn skills that will help you improve any kind of writing: paragraphs, essays, short stories, reports, and research papers.

The References section at the end of the worktext contains the original sentences by professional writers used as models in the practices throughout the worktext. Don't consider them the answers in the back of the book, as in a math textbook.

When you look up the original sentences you may decide that the professionally written sentence is better than yours; if so, study the difference. You may, however, decide that yours is just as good; if so, congratulate yourself. You may even decide that yours is better; in that case, take a bow.

1

Practicing Sentence-Composing Techniques

> "Because I remained in the third form [grade] three times as long as anyone else, I had three times as much of sentence analysis, learned it thoroughly, and thus got into my bones the structure of the English sentence. The essential structure of the ordinary English sentence is a noble thing."
>
> *Winston Churchill*

When you write sentences and when professional writers write sentences, the results are often different. A big difference is variety in the structure of sentences. The goal of *Sentence Composing for College* is to bridge the gap.

In this worktext, you'll practice four sentence-composing techniques to learn to write sentences similar in structure to those of professional writers: *sentence unscrambling*, *sentence imitating*, *sentence combining*, and *sentence expanding*.

You'll learn from the professional writers themselves, who serve as mentors in your apprenticeship in sentence improvement, how to build better sentences.

The study of the sentence has too often been neglected as a way of improving writing; instead the sentence was used mainly for analyzing grammar. *Sentence Composing for College* studies the sentence as a way of improving your writing.

In studying good sentence structure you are learning about the backbone of writing paragraphs, essays, short stories, reports, research papers.

All writing equals the sum of its sentences.

Focus 1

Sentence Unscrambling

Sentence unscrambling simply means putting mixed-up sentence parts back together to make a meaningful, well-written sentence. Sentence unscrambling permits a close look at how professional writers assemble the parts of their sentences.

The sentence parts are listed in a different order from that in the original sentence. To illustrate, here's an original sentence, a list with the sentence parts in the same order as in the original, and a list with the sentence parts scrambled.

Original Sentence

When his father, who was old and twisted with toil, made over to him the ownership of the farm and seemed content to creep away to a corner and wait for death, he shrugged his shoulders and dismissed the old man from his mind.

Sherwood Anderson, Winesburg, Ohio

Original Order

1. When his father,

2. who was old

3. and twisted with toil,

4. made over to him the ownership

5. of the farm

6. and seemed content

7. to creep away

8. to a corner

9. and wait for death,

10. he shrugged his shoulders

11. and dismissed the old man

12. from his mind.

Scrambled Order

1. to a corner
2. from his mind.
3. and wait for death,
4. When his father,
5. he shrugged his shoulders
6. made over to him the ownership
7. who was old
8. and dismissed the old man
9. of the farm
10. and twisted with toil,
11. to creep away
12. and seemed content

Practice 1

To recognize that sentence parts are movable, do the following Practice. For each list of scrambled sentence parts, unscramble the parts three times, each time producing a sentence with the parts in a different order. Punctuate accordingly. Indicate which of the three versions you consider the most effective arrangement, and explain your choice. Then check the References on page 157 to compare your choices with the sentences as originally written.

Example

Scrambled Sentence Parts

a. so coldly burning
b. falling upon his knees
c. which was so huge
d. as he watched the star
e. he began to pray humbly

Unscrambled Sentences (three versions)

1. Falling upon his knees as he watched the star, which was so huge, so coldly burning, he began to pray humbly.

2. He began to pray humbly, falling upon his knees, as he watched the star, which was so huge, so coldly burning.

3. As he watched the star, which was so huge, so coldly burning, falling upon his knees, he began to pray humbly.

The most effective version is the first. The second is less well organized, with the main actions (praying, falling on his knees) appearing secondary to the description of the star. The third version places the phrase *falling upon his knees* in a position in which it seems to describe the star rather than the person.

1a. leaving the oak box of money

 b. leaving the quirt

 c. he ran from the place

 d. leaving his suitcase

John Steinbeck, East of Eden

2a. a mortgage financier

 b. the father was respectable and tight

 c. and forecloser

 d. and a stern, upright collection-plate passer

O. Henry, "The Ransom of Red Chief"

3a. for nothing can be done

 b. after Buck Fanshaw's inquest

 c. without a public meeting

 d. a meeting of the short-haired brotherhood was held

 e. on the Pacific coast

 f. and an expression of sentiment

Mark Twain, "Buck Fanshaw's Funeral"

4a.   the littlest

  b.   with them

  c.   I had ever seen

  d.   carrying a gnarled walking stick

  e.   oldest man

  f.   was Elmo Goodhue Pipgrass

Max Shulman, "The Unlucky Winner"

5a.   over long woolen underwear

  b.   he bounded

  c.   around his chest

  d.   out of bed

  e.   and a leather jacket

  f.   wearing a long flannel nightgown

  g.   a nightcap

James Thurber, "The Night the Ghost Got In"

6a.   looked up from his scrambled eggs

  b.   once upon a sunny morning

  c.   who sat in a breakfast nook

  d.   quietly cropping the roses

  e.   with a gold horn

  f.   a man

  g.   to see a white unicorn

  h.   in the garden

James Thurber, "The Unicorn in the Garden"

7a.   grabbed my right foot

  b.   of patent-leather dancing pumps

  c.   then

  d.   and shoved it into one of them

e.   as a shoehorn

f.   she removed the gleaming pair

g.   out of a box on the bed

h.   using her finger
     Jean Shepherd, "Wanda Hickey's Night of Golden Memories"

Practice 2

Part One: Each list below, when unscrambled, will become one of the sentences in a paragraph from Michael Crichton's *Jurassic Park*. In that paragraph, a tyrannosaur attacks, during a thunderstorm, a Land Cruiser (car) containing two children, a brother and sister. Unscramble the lists to produce the four sentences in the paragraph. In each list, the sentence part that begins the sentence is capitalized. Answers are in the References on pages 157–158.

1a. with a muddy splash

 b. The rear of the car

 c. and then it thumped down

 d. into the air for a moment

 e. lifted up

2a. of the car

 b. Then it moved

 c. around the side

3a. that blended with the thunder

 b. At the back

 c. a deep rumbling growl

 d. the animal snorted

4a. out of all the side windows

 b. The big raised tail

 c. blocked their view

5a. mounted on the back of the Land Cruiser

b. and,

c. It sank its jaws into the spare tire

d. tore it away

e. in a single head shake,

After unscrambling the sentences, arrange the sentences according to this outline to produce a meaningful paragraph:

Sentence 1:   approach by animal

Sentence 2:   car windows blocked

Sentence 3:   sounds of animal

Sentence 4:   attack to part of car

Sentence 5:   lifting of car

Write out and punctuate the paragraph.

Part Two: Each list below, when unscrambled, will become one of the sentences in a paragraph from Edgar Allan Poe's "The Fall of the House of Usher." In that paragraph, the mysterious main character Lady Madeline of Usher is described. Unscramble the lists to produce the four sentences in the paragraph. In each list, the sentence part that begins the sentence is capitalized.

1a. there did stand the lofty and enshrouded figure

b. but then without those doors

c. It was the work of the rushing gust—

d. of the Lady Madeline of Usher

2a. and the evidence of some bitter struggle

b. There was blood

c. upon every portion of her emaciated frame

d. upon her white robes

3a. there had been found the potency of a spell,

b.   upon the instant, their ponderous and ebony jaws

c.   As if in the superhuman energy of his utterance

d.   the huge antique panels

e.   to which the speaker pointed

f.   threw slowly back,

4a.   to and fro upon the threshold—

b.   bore him to the floor a corpse,

c.   then, with a low, moaning cry,

d.   and in her violent and now final death-agonies,

e.   For a moment she remained trembling and reeling

f.   fell heavily inward upon the person of her brother,

g.   and a victim to the terrors he had anticipated

After unscrambling the sentences, arrange the sentences according to this outline to produce a meaningful paragraph:

Sentence 1:   setting the stage

Sentence 2:   introduction of Lady Madeline

Sentence 3:   description of Lady Madeline

Sentence 4:   action of Lady Madeline

Write out and punctuate the paragraph.

Practice 3

In the paragraphs below, practice sentence variety by moving sentence parts to new positions. Change the position of underlined sentence parts to a place that is equally effective. Write out the new paragraphs.

1. <u>As quickly as it had come</u>, the wind died, and the clearing was quiet again. The heron stood in the shallows, <u>motionless and waiting</u>. A little water snake swam up the pool, <u>turning its periscope head from side to side</u>.

   John Steinbeck, Of Mice and Men

2. Behind us was the town of Castle Rock, <u>spread out on the long hill that was known as Castle View</u>, surrounding its green and shady common. <u>Further down Castle River</u> you could see the stacks of the woolen mill spewing smoke into a sky the color of gunmetal and spewing waste into the water. The Jolly Furniture Barn was on our left, and straight ahead of us were the railroad tracks, <u>bright and heliographing in the sun</u>.

   Stephen King, "The Body"

3. <u>Standing at the front window and holding back the curtain</u>, Agatha watched for the first star. In the summertime she had to be alert <u>because the sky stayed light for so long that the stars would more or less melt into view</u>. Sometimes Thomas waited, too. He said his wishes aloud, <u>no matter how often she warned him not to</u>. He wished for definite objects—toys and candy and such—<u>as if the sky were one big Sears, Roebuck catalog</u>. Agatha, <u>on the other hand</u>, wished silently, and not even in words. She wished <u>in a strong wash of feeling</u>.

   Anne Tyler, Saint Maybe

4. We paid our dollars <u>at the admission gate</u> and threw ourselves into the carnival <u>like famished beggars at a feast</u>. The strings of light bulbs gleamed <u>over our heads like trapped stars</u>. A lot of kids our age were there, <u>along with their parents</u>, and some older people and high school kids, too. <u>Around us</u> the rides grunted, clattered, and rattled. We bought our tickets and got on the Ferris wheel, and I made the mistake of sitting with Davy Ray. <u>When we got to the very top and the wheel paused to allow riders on the bottommost gondola</u>, he grinned and started rocking us back and forth and yelling that the bolts were about to come loose.

   Robert R. McCammon, Boy's Life

Practice 4

From your own writing, choose several paragraphs to practice sentence variety by rearranging the sentence parts in your sentences. Identify the parts of the sentences that can be rearranged, and then rewrite those sentences, moving those parts to new places.

*F*ocus 2

Sentence Imitating

Sentence imitating is the use of professional writers' sentences as models for writing your own sentences. The structure of your sentence is the same as the model's, but the content is different. The purpose is to increase your ability to vary sentence structure through a deliberate imitation of the structure of the model sentence.

Practice 1

Below are groups of three sentences. Two of the sentences in each group are identical in structure. The other sentence in the group, although competently written, is structurally different from the other two. Identify the sentence that is different. Answers are in the References on pages 158–159.

1a. Great was his care of them.

 b. Something else he saw.

 c. Chilling was her story of passion.

2a. The big thing, exciting yet frightening, was to talk to her, say what he hoped to do.

 b. There was also a rhino, who, from the tracks and the kicked-up mound of strawy dung, came there each night.

 c. An acceptable solution, simple and efficient, is to negotiate with the management, emphasize what the workers want to delete.

3a. Much later the accountant finished, ledgers in their vertical files on the right side of the desk, pencils and pens in their containers decorated with seals and designs on the shelf above the desk.

 b. This leader, whose word was law among the boys who defied authority for the sake of defiance, was no more than twelve or thirteen years old and looked even younger.

c. Soon afterwards they retired, Mama in her big oak bed on one side of the room, Emilio and Rosy in their boxes full of straw and sheepskins on the other side of the room.

4a. During rush-hour traffic, when his nerves were frazzled, Brent Hammond, twenty miles above the speed limit, hit his brakes, from which came sharp peals and leaden grindings as though the metal were alive and hurting.

b. On stormy nights, when the tide was out, the bay of Fougere, fifty feet below the house, resembled an immense black pit, from which arose mutterings and sighs as if the sands down there had been alive and complaining.

c. Aleck Sander stood out from the shadows, walking, already quite near in the moonless dark, a little taller than Big Ed, though there was only a few months' difference between them.

5a. Listening to evaluate the difference between the two violins, the concertmaster chose, glancing back and forth over the two instruments, the one with the slightly arched bow.

b. Light flickered on bits of ruby glass and on sensitive capillary hairs in the nylon-brushed nostrils of the creature that quivered gently, gently, its eight legs spidered under it on rubber-padded paws.

c. Pretending to take an interest in the New Season's Models, Gumbril made, squinting sideways over the burning tip of his cigar, an inventory of her features.

6a. He reached over for the submachine gun, took the clip out that was in the magazine, felt in his pockets for the clips, opened the action and looked through the barrel, put the clip back in the groove of the magazine until it clicked, and then looked down the hill slope.

b. Amused yet bewildered, near the sarcastic boy in a corner of the cafeteria, with a friend who had invited her and another whose boyfriend was his remarkably opposite twin, Joan thought constantly that noon about the ambivalence of her emotions.

c. Abandoned and helpless, under the crude lean-to in the courtyard of the tin factory, beside the woman who had lost a breast and the man whose burned face was scarcely a face any more, Miss Sasaki suffered awfully that night from the pain in her broken leg.

Practice 2

Compare these two sentences: the first is a model; the second, an imitation. Notice how the imitation relied on the clues (**boldface**) of punctuation and certain kinds of words and word endings.

Example

Model: Pretend**ing to** take an interest in **the** New Season's Models, Gumbril made, squinting sideways **over** the burning tip of his cigar, an inventory of her features.

Aldous Huxley, Antic Hay

Imitation: Listen**ing to** evaluate the difference between **the** two violins, the concertmaster chose, glanc**ing** back and forth **over** the two instruments, the one with the slightly arched bow.

Review the punctuation patterns in the model and the imitation. They are identical. In doing the imitation, the student worked on one sentence part at a time, concentrating on how that particular sentence part is structured, then imitated only that particular sentence part. The process is then repeated with the next sentence part, then the next, the next, and so forth.

First Sentence Part

Model: Pretending to take an interest in the New Season's Models,
Imitation: Listening to evaluate the difference between the two violins,

Second Sentence Part

Model: Gumbril made,
Imitation: the concertmaster chose,

Third Sentence Part

Model: squinting sideways over the burning tip of his cigar,
Imitation: glancing back and forth over the two instruments,

Fourth Sentence Part

Model: an inventory of her features.
Imitation: the one with the slightly arched bow.

Notice that the two sentences are almost identical in structure; however, they are very different in content and somewhat different in length—the imitation uses more words. Duplicating the exact number of words in the model is not necessary. Don't focus on the words; focus, instead, on the structure.

Following the guidelines for sentence imitating mentioned earlier, write an imitation of each of these model sentences.

1. Great was his care of them.

   Jack London, "All Gold Cañon"

2. The big thing, exciting yet frightening, was to talk to her, say what he hoped to do.

   Bernard Malamud, The Assistant

3. He had never been hungrier, and he filled his mouth with wine, faintly tarry-tasting from the leather bag, and swallowed.

   Ernest Hemingway, For Whom the Bell Tolls

4. Soon afterwards they retired, Mama in her big oak bed on one side of the room, Emilio and Rosy in their boxes full of straw and sheepskins on the other side of the room.

   John Steinbeck, "Flight"

5. On stormy nights, when the tide was out, the bay of Fougere, fifty feet below the house, resembled an immense black pit, from which arose mutterings and sighs as if the sands down there had been alive and complaining.

   Joseph Conrad, "The Idiots"

Here are sample imitations of the five model sentences above.

1. Chilling was her story of passion.

2. An acceptable solution, simple and efficient, is to negotiate with the management, emphasize what the workers want to delete.

3. The horse had never been nastier, and it threw its riders to the ground, cold and hard from the frost, and bolted.

4. Much later the accountant finished, ledgers in their vertical files on the right side of the desk, pencils and pens in their containers decorated with seals and designs on the shelf above the desk.

5. During rush-hour traffic, when his nerves were frazzled, Brent Hammond, twenty miles above the speed limit, hit his brakes, from which came sharp peals and leaden grindings as though the metal were alive and hurting.

Practice 3

From the two sentences (a and b) following each model sentence, select the one that imitates the sentence structure of the model; then write your own imitation of the model. All models are from *The Martian Chronicles* by Ray Bradbury.

1. One minute it was Ohio winter, with doors closed, windows locked, the panes blind with frost, icicles fringing every roof, children skiing on slopes, housewives lumbering like great black bears in their furs along the icy streets.

a. Near the race track where the Derby was held, a peanut vendor, with wrinkled skin, a face like an eagle, boldly stood almost directly in the line of the huge traffic, hawking his peanuts, describing their superb taste, rich aroma.

b. Yesterday it was the Boston Marathon, with crowds gathered, police ready, the runners covered with suntan oils, many limbering up, even wheelchair participants checking their equipment like careful auto mechanics with their tools of all sorts.

2. Named but unnamed and borrowing from humans everything but humanity, the robots stared at the nailed lids of their labeled F.O.B. boxes, in a death that was not even a death, for there had never been a life.

a. With the carousel slide projector carefully placed atop several books to provide the right height for perfect screen projection, with the slides placed within it, the right organization for the presentation, the lesson began.

b. Hesitant but not uncertain, and drawing from libraries all of her knowledge, she walked into the room for her comprehensive examination, with a feeling that was certainly not calm, because there would always be the unknown.

3. Here and there a fire, forgotten in the last rush, lingered and in a sudden excess of strength fed upon the dry bones of some littered shack.

a. Once or twice the siren, obscured by the sudden explosion, echoed but with a dreadful parody of itself sounded with a noise like a banshee.

b. Now and then, he tweaked his painted, bulbous nose, and the children nearby giggled at the bicycle-horn sound.

Practice 4

Write an imitation of each of the model sentences below.

1. One of these dogs, the best one, had disappeared.
   Fred Gipson, Old Yeller

2. Among the company was a lawyer, a young man of about twenty-five.
   Anton Chekhov, "The Bet"

3. Halfway there he heard the sound he dreaded, the hollow, rasping cough of a horse.
   John Steinbeck, The Red Pony

4. Poppa, a good quiet man, spent the last hours before our parting moving aimlessly about the yard, keeping to himself and avoiding me.

      Gordon Parks, "My Mother's Dream for Me"

5. Standing in the truck bed, holding onto the bars of the sides, rode the others, twelve-year-old Ruthie and ten-year-old Winfield, grime-faced and wild, their eyes tired but excited, their fingers and the edges of their mouths black and sticky from licorice whips, whined out of their father in town.

      John Steinbeck, The Grapes of Wrath

Practice 5

For each of the four model sentences below, there are two sentence imitations. Each of the sentence imitations approximates the structure of the model. First, match the imitations for each model. Next, write an imitation of each model.

Models

1. Near the spot upriver to which Mr. Tanimoto had transported the priests, there sat a large case of rice cakes which a rescue party had evidently brought for the wounded lying thereabouts but hadn't distributed.

      John Hersey, Hiroshima

2. There was also a rhino, who, from the tracks and the kicked-up mound of strawy dung, came there each night.

      Ernest Hemingway, Green Hills of Africa

3. The dark silence was there and the heavy shapes, sitting, and the little blue light burning.

      Ray Bradbury, The Vintage Bradbury

4. Light flickered on bits of ruby glass and on sensitive capillary hairs in the nylon-brushed nostrils of the creature that quivered gently, gently, its eight legs spidered under it on rubber-padded paws.

      Ray Bradbury, Fahrenheit 451

Imitations

a. Stars twinkled on pieces of broken shells and on ruined sand castles in the sea-drenched sand of the beach that stretched miles, endless miles, its many shells strewn on it by high-crested waves.

b. At the place in the room where he had left his books, there was a stack of journals that had evidently been brought by several of the more academic students but hadn't been used by the teacher.

c. The dense fog was there and the bloody bodies, dying, and the torn white flag waving.

d. I sat on velvet grass and under spreading blue leaves in the light-yellow atmosphere of a planet that orbited, slowly, steadily, its six moons clinging close like newborn children.

e. There was also a turtle, who, from the half-eaten tomato and the hole under the fence, had visited the garden that day.

f. The big race was next and the line of cars, waiting, and the red flag ready.

g. There was also the horror, which, from the odor and snake-belly sensation of dead flesh, came there each time.

h. Outside the shack from which the patrol had started shooting, there was a blast of gunfire that the rebels had intended for the door lock but hadn't hit.

Practice 6

Identify three imitations of the model paragraph.

Model Paragraph

This is a snail shell, round, full, and glossy as a horse chestnut. Comfortable and compact, it sits curled up like a cat in the hollow of my hand. Milky and opaque, it has the pinkish bloom of the sky on a summer evening, ripening to rain. On its smooth, symmetrical face is pencilled with precision a perfect spiral, winding inward to the pin point center of the shell, the tiny dark core of the apex, the pupil of the eye. It stares at me, this mysterious single eye—and I stare back.

Anne Morrow Lindbergh, Gift from the Sea

Paragraph 1

The school bus pulled up and let the children out. One of the little boys was running after his dog. The dog had followed him to school and refused to go home when the boy chased him. The other students thought it was funny when the dog ran into the school building. Somebody had left the door open on purpose.

Paragraph 2

When it snowed yesterday, I was at the library. The library is one near where I live and has many books that can help a lot with the assignments from school. A lot of my friends go there to visit with each other and to do some research and studying. The librarians are helpful when you need to find some books to do a history or English assignment. I like the library!

Paragraph 3

There is a snowflake, light, delicate, and fluffy as a piece of cotton. Swirling and blowing, it floats down from the sky like the seeds of the milkweed plant. White and bright, it has the gleam of the blinding sunlight and the reflecting moonlight, shining in silver. On its surface is stenciled a star, formed with its five or six symmetrical points, the arms of the snowflake, the body of it. It falls to earth, this crystal of beauty—and the earth melts it.

Paragraph 4

This is an old book, interesting, long, but thought-provoking as a philosophical treatise. Soiled but well read, it remains standing upright on my bookshelf mixed in with paperbacks. Analytic and probing, it reveals many pitfalls in the process of thinking, describing wrong conclusions. In its yellow pages are recorded with skill many criticisms, converging ultimately into the story of all people, the universal, timeless tale of every individual, the discourse on humanity. It speaks of man, this lengthy discourse— yet man ignores it.

Paragraph 5

Some rock stars are very colorful and exciting to watch when they perform at a live concert. Usually hundreds or thousands of teenagers attend these concerts, which are usually held in large convention halls or sometimes outdoors in large parks or other public places. Music-lovers look forward to attending these exciting events. Despite what many people say, the behavior at the concerts is very good. It is noisy, but since noise is what anyone would expect at such concerts, nobody there really minds.

Paragraph 6

This is a room, dark, comfortable, and at times lonely as a silent cave. Small and private, it can absorb my thoughts like a sponge. Comfortable and secure, the room has a feeling of safety and peace, providing a hiding place. On its walls are varicolored posters, all reflecting moods of mine, ranging from joy to despair. The posters face me, those mirrors of my soul— and I reminisce.

Practice 7

Write a description that imitates the model paragraph.

Practice 8

Write an original paragraph five to ten sentences in length. Include somewhere in the paragraph a sentence imitation of as many of the following model sentences as you can. Even if you use only one or two model sentences for imitation, in the rest of your paragraph try to write sentences (without the use of models) that are similar in structure to those associated with professional writing.

1. Over this rocky area relieved by a few shady tall persimmon trees the graduating class walked.
   Maya Angelou, I Know Why the Caged Bird Sings

2. A few hours before, he adored me, was devoted and worshipful, and now he was angry.
   Anaïs Nin, The Diary of Anaïs Nin

3. Behind a billboard, on an empty lot, he opened the purse and saw a pile of silver and copper coins.
   Charlie Chaplin, My Autobiography

4. The frozen earth thawed, leaving the short grass looking wet and weary.

   Peter Abrahams, Tell Freedom

5. I was fourteen at the time, too young for a full-time job, but I managed to get a Bronx Home News route, for which I was paid five dollars a week.

   Milton Kaplan, Commentary

6. In my robe and barefoot in the backyard, under cover of going to see about my new beans, I gave myself up to the gentle warmth and thanked God that no matter what evil I had done in my life He had allowed me to live to see this day.

   Maya Angelou, I Know Why the Caged Bird Sings

*F*ocus 3

Sentence Combining

Sentence combining is the process of blending two or more related sentences into one sentence. Unlike sentence unscrambling and sentence imitating, in which you were given the structure for the sentence parts, sentence combining provides only the content. You provide the sentence structure in which to express that content.

Before combining sentences, try decombining them. Decombining professionally written sentences provides much insight into good writing. Here are three examples:

Sentence Decombining: Short Sentence

Silently, desperately, he fought with all his weapons.
Katherine Anne Porter, Ship of Fools

1. It was done silently.

2. It was done desperately.

3. He fought.

4. The fighting was done with weapons.

5. All of the weapons were used.

6. All of the weapons were his.

Sentence Decombining: Medium Sentence

Once his back happened to be half turned toward the door, and, hearing a noise there, he wheeled and sprang up, uttering a loud cry.
Stephen Crane, "The Blue Hotel"

1. Once something happened.

2. What happened was that his back happened to be half turned.

3. His back was half turned toward the door.

4. During this time he heard a noise there.

5. Upon hearing it, he wheeled.

6. Upon hearing it, he sprang up.

7. During the wheeling and the springing up, he was doing something.

8. He was uttering a loud cry.

Sentence Decombining: Long Sentence

He backed Jack up against the ropes, measured him and then hooked the left very light to the side of Jack's head and socked the right into the body as hard as he could sock, just as low as he could get it.

Ernest Hemingway, "Fifty Grand"

1. He backed Jack up.

2. The backing was against the ropes.

3. He measured him.

4. Then he hooked the left.

5. The hook was very light.

6. The hook was to the side of the head.

7. The head was Jack's.

8. He socked the right.

9. He socked it into the body.

10. The socking was as hard as he could sock.

11. The socking was just as low as he could get it.

Practice 1

Decombine each of the sentences below. The number of sentences you can list is not fixed. Try for more rather than fewer sentences. In doing so, you'll become more conscious of the greater economy, variety, and maturity of the original sentence.

1. The fixer got up on his raw hands and bleeding knees and went on, blindly crawling across the yard.

      Bernard Malamud, The Fixer

2. She flicked her wrist neatly out of Doctor Harry's pudgy careful fingers and pulled the sheet up to her chin.

      Katherine Anne Porter, "The Jilting of Granny Weatherall"

3. On the table, covered with oilcloth figured with clusters of blue grapes, a place was set, and he smelled hot coffee-cake of some kind.

      Willa Cather, "Neighbor Rosicky"

4. She cleared away the smoking things, then drew back the cotton bedspread from the bed she had been sitting on, took off her slippers, and got into bed.

      J. D. Salinger, Franny and Zooey

5. The driver of the car stopped it, slamming it to a skidding halt on the greasy pavement without warning, actually flinging the two passengers forward until they caught themselves with their braced hands against the dash.

      William Faulkner, "Delta Autumn"

Practice 2

Each of the lists of sentences below was derived from a single sentence by a professional writer. Combine all of the sentences into just one sentence, following the order of the list. Punctuate correctly. After you complete each one, compare your sentence with the original in the References on page 160.

1a. The boy watched.

  b. During the watching, his eyes did something.

  c. His eyes were bulging.

  d. All of this occurred in the dark.

      From *Edmund Ware,* "An Underground Episode"

2a.   One of the dogs had done something.

   b.   This dog was the best one of all the dogs.

   c.   It had disappeared.
From *Fred Gipson*, Old Yeller

3a.   Doctor Parcival was jumping to his feet.

   b.   At the same time he was breaking off the tale.

   c.   Doctor Parcival began to walk up and down.

   d.   The office in which he walked was of the *Winesburg Eagle*.

   e.   In that office was where someone sat.

   f.   The someone was George Willard.

   g.   As George sat, he was listening.
From *Sherwood Anderson*, Winesburg, Ohio

4a.   This land was waterless.

   b.   It was furred with cacti.

   c.   The cacti could store water.

   d.   In addition, the land was furred with the great-rooted brush.

   e.   The brush could reach deep into the earth.

   f.   The brush would do this for a little moisture.

   g.   The brush could get along on very little moisture.
From *John Steinbeck*, The Pearl

5a.   It glided through.

   b.   As it glided, it brushed the twigs.

   c.   The twigs were overhanging.

   d.   In addition, it disappeared from the river.

e. It disappeared like some creature.

f. The creature was slim.

g. The creature was amphibious.

h. The creature was leaving the water.

i. The creature was leaving for its lair.

j. The lair was in the forests.

From *Joseph Conrad, "The Lagoon"*

Practice 3

Combine each list of sentences twice to produce two different versions to practice variety. You needn't necessarily stick to the order of ideas in the list. You may use any arrangement you think will produce a good sentence. Compare your best sentences with the authors' in the References on page 160. Which are better? Why?

1a. The house was most enjoyable.

b. The house was in the country.

c. The enjoyment of the house was on a particular afternoon.

d. The afternoon was wintry.

From *James Thurber, "The Owl in the Attic"*

2a. The earth was bloody in the setting light.

b. The bloodiness was caused by the sun.

c. The sun was setting.

d. At the same time, the truck came back.

From *John Steinbeck*, The Grapes of Wrath

3a. He moves nervously.

b. He moves fast.

c. His movement, however, has a restraint.

    d.   The restraint suggests that he is a cautious man.

    e.   The restraint suggests that he is a thoughtful man.
From John Hersey, Hiroshima

4a.   The girls stood aside.

    b.   The very small children rolled in the dust.

    c.   Some children clung to the hands of their older brothers or sisters.

    d.   The girls were doing two things.

    e.   They looked over their shoulders at the boys.

    f.   They talked among themselves.
From Shirley Jackson, "The Lottery"

5a.   The cake was shaped in a frying pan.

    b.   He took flour.

    c.   He took oil.

    d.   He shaped them into a cake.

    e.   The stove functioned on gas.

    f.   The gas was bottled.

    g.   He lighted the stove.

    h.   The stove was little.
From Albert Camus, "The Guest"

Practice 4

In this Practice, combine the sentences in the lists using the fewest possible words to practice economy. The number of words in the author's sentence is indicated. Don't worry about using that exact number, but try not to exceed it by much. Compare your sentences with the originals in the References on pages 160–161.

1a.   He distributed handbills for merchants.

    b.   He did this, and the following activities, from ages ten to fifteen.

c.   He held horses.

d.   He ran confidential errands.

Word Count: 15

From *Thornton Wilder*, The Bridge of San Luis Rey

2a. Nick looked down into the water.

b.   The water was clear.

c.   The water was brown.

d.   The brown color came from the pebbly bottom.

e.   As Nick looked down he watched the trout.

f.   The trout were keeping themselves steady in the current.

g.   They kept themselves steady with their fins.

h.   Their fins were wavering.

Word Count: 25

From *Ernest Hemingway, "Big Two-Hearted River"*

3a. On one side was a tiny meadow.

b.   The meadow began at the very lip of the pool.

c.   The meadow had a surface of green.

d.   The surface was cool.

e.   The surface was resilient.

f.   The surface extended.

g.   The surface extended to the base.

h.   The base was of the browning wall.

Word Count: 30

From *Jack London, "All Gold Cañon"*

4a. In the stillness of the air many things in the forest seemed to have been bewitched.

b.   They were bewitched into an immobility.

c. The immobility was perfect.

d. The immobility was final.

e. Every tree seemed bewitched.

f. Every leaf seemed bewitched.

g. Every bough seemed bewitched.

h. Every tendril of creeper seemed bewitched.

i. Every petal of minute blossoms seemed bewitched.

Word Count: 33 (long sentence)

From *Joseph Conrad, "The Lagoon"*

Practice 5

Combine sentences to create paragraphs. The number of words contained in the original sentence is indicated. Approximate it. Try for clear meaning, word economy, and sentence variety. Compare your results with the originals in the References on page 161.

Paragraph 1

Narration of a bull fight from "The Undefeated" by Ernest Hemingway:

1a. Manuel waved his hand.

b. Manuel was leaning against the barrera.

c. Manuel was watching the bull.

d. And the gypsy ran out.

e. The gypsy was trailing his cape.

Word Count: 19 (medium sentence)

2a. The bull pivoted.

b. The bull was in full gallop.

c.   And the bull charged the cape.

d.   The bull's head was down.

e.   The bull's tail was rising.

Word Count: 16 (medium sentence)

3a.   The gypsy moved.

b.   The movement was in a zigzag.

c.   And as he passed, the bull caught sight of him.

d.   The bull abandoned the cape.

e.   The reason for the abandonment was to charge the man.

Word Count: 24 (medium sentence)

4a.   The gypsy sprinted and vaulted the red fence.

b.   The red fence was of the barrera.

c.   As the gypsy sprinted and vaulted, the bull struck something.

d.   The bull struck the red fence of the barrera.

e.   The bull struck it with his horns.

Word Count: 19 (medium sentence)

5a.   He tossed into it with his horns.

b.   He tossed into it twice.

c.   He was banging into the wood.

d.   He was banging blindly.

Word Count: 13 (short sentence)

Paragraph 2

Description and explanation of a native African bushman dance from *The Harmless People* by Elizabeth Marshall Thomas:

1a.   To have a dance the women do certain things.

b.   They sit in a circle.

   c.   Their babies are on their backs.

   d.   Their babies are asleep.

   e.   The women sing medicine songs.

   f.   The songs are sung in several parts.

   g.   The songs are sung in falsetto voices.

   h.   During the singing the women clap their hands.

   i.   The clapping is done in rhythm.

   j.   The rhythm is sharp.

   k.   The rhythm is staccato.

   l.   The rhythm is at counterpoint to the rhythm of their voices.

Word Count: 43 (long sentence)

2a.   Behind their backs the men dance.

   b.   The men dance one behind the other.

   c.   The men circle slowly around.

   d.   The men take steps.

   e.   The steps are very short.

   f.   The steps are pounding.

   g.   The steps are at counterpoint to both the rhythms.

   h.   One of the rhythms is the rhythm of the singing.

   i.   The other rhythm is the rhythm of the clapping.

Word Count: 33 (long sentence)

3a.   Now and then the men do two things.

   b.   They, sing, too.

   c.   They sing in their deeper voices.

   d.   Another thing they do is use their dance rattles.

   e.   Their rattles are made from dry cocoons.

f.   The cocoons are strung together with sinew cords.

g.   Their dance rattles are tied to their legs.

h.   Their dance rattles add a sharp, high clatter.

i.   The high clatter is like the sound of shaken gourds.

j.   The rattling sound is very well timed.

k.   The good timing is because the men step accurately.

Word Count: 49 (long sentence)

4a.   A Bushman dance is a pattern.

b.   The pattern is infinitely complicated.

c.   The pattern consists of two things.

d.   One thing is of voices.

e.   The other thing is of rhythm.

f.   The pattern is an orchestra of bodies.

g.   The pattern is making music that has two characteristics.

h.   One characteristic is that the music is infinitely varied.

i.   The other characteristic is that the music is always precise.

Word Count: 25 (medium sentence)

Practice 6

Here, the sentence breaks aren't indicated. For each paragraph:

1. Decide how many sentences to combine into just one sentence. Do this by combining all sentences that have related content and arranging the content in the best order.

2. Vary the sentence lengths (short, medium, and long) as we as the structures.

The number of words and sentences contained in the author's paragraph is indicated. Use it as a rough guideline. You need not stick to the order of the content in the list of sentences. Use any order that is smooth and logical. Compare your paragraphs with the originals in the References on page 162.

Paragraph 1

Description of a Victorian house from *The Martian Chronicles* by Ray Bradbury. (The author's paragraph has 90 words and four sentences.)

1. Outside stood an iron deer.

2. It stood upon this lawn.

3. Further up on the green stood a Victorian house.

4. The house was tall.

5. The house was brown.

6. The house was quiet in the sunlight.

7. The house was all covered with scrolls and rococo.

8. The house's windows were made of blue colored glass.

9. The house's windows were made of pink colored glass.

10. The house's windows were made of yellow colored glass.

11. The house's windows were made of green colored glass.

12. Upon the porch were two things.

13. One was geraniums.

14. The geraniums were hairy.

15. The other was a swing.

16. The swing was old.

17. The swing was hooked into the porch ceiling.

18. The swing now swung back and forth, back and forth.

19. The swinging occurred in a little breeze.

20. A cupola was at the summit of the house.

21. The cupola had diamond leaded-glass windows.

22. The cupola had a dunce-cap roof!

Paragraph 2

A scene at dusk from *Winesburg, Ohio* by Sherwood Anderson. (The author's paragraph has 134 words and five sentences.)

1. Upon the veranda a man walked up and down.

2. He was little.

3. He was fat.

4. He walked nervously.

5. The veranda was half decayed.

6. The veranda was of a small frame house.

7. The house stood near the edge of a ravine.

8. The ravine was near the town of Winesburg, Ohio.

9. The man could see the public highway.

10. He could see the highway across a long field.

11. The field had been seeded for clover.

12. But it had produced only a dense crop of weeds.

13. The weeds were yellow mustard weeds.

14. A wagon went along the public highway.

15. The wagon was filled with berry pickers.

16. The berry pickers were returning from the fields.

17. The berry pickers were youths.

18. The berry pickers were maidens.

19. The berry pickers laughed.

20. The berry pickers shouted.

21. They shouted boisterously.

22. A boy leaped from the wagon.

23. The boy was clad in a shirt.

24. The shirt was blue.

25. The boy attempted to drag after him one of the maidens.

26. The maiden screamed.

27. The maiden protested.

28. She protested shrilly.

29. The feet of the boy in the road kicked up a cloud.

30. The cloud was of dust.

31. The dust cloud floated across the face of the sun.

32. The sun was departing.

Practice 7

Select two paragraphs, each at least ten sentences in length, from a piece of writing you've recently done. The paragraphs may be from the same piece of writing or from two different ones. For each paragraph, using sentence combining, reduce the ten sentences to seven or fewer. In the revised sentences, aim for variety of sentence structure and length.

*F*ocus 4

Sentence Expanding

Sentence expanding is a process for changing your sentences into sentences like those of professional writers. It transforms reduced sentences into fully developed sentences.

Example

Reduced Sentence
There stood two squat old-fashioned decanters of cut glass.

Expanded Sentence
In the centre of the table there stood, as sentries to a fruit-stand which upheld a pyramid of oranges and American apples, two squat old-fashioned decanters of cut glass, one containing port and the other dark sherry.

James Joyce, "The Dead"

Compare this version, a rewrite of the original, with Joyce's original sentence:

Two squat old-fashioned decanters stood there. They were in the centre of the table. They were like sentries to a fruit-stand near them. The fruit-stand upheld a pyramid of oranges and American apples. One of the decanters contained port. The other one contained sherry.

The rewrite is uneconomical, using six sentences to express what Joyce did in just one sentence; it uses 44 words to Joyce's 37. It's poorly organized, failing to show as clearly as Joyce's the interrelationships among the various objects described. It's uninteresting, beginning each of the six sentences in the same monotonous way.

Can an expanded sentence, like a balloon filled to over-capacity, "burst"? As long as a sentence is clear in meaning, it's not over-expanded, regardless of how many words are in the sentence, regardless of how many different structures are present, regardless of how many ideas are packed into it. Among American writers, William Faulkner is famous for the ultralong sentences that characterize his style. The French writer Victor Hugo is often cited as having written one of the longest sentences ever, one that has hundreds of words, in *Les Miserables*. The Irish writer James Joyce went even further, ending his novel *Ulysses* with a sentence that runs over twenty pages!

Even among professional writers, however, such ultralong sentences are rare. Still, on the average, sentences by professional writers are longer than those by students.

Practice 1

To practice adding expansions, substitute new ones for those in boldface.

Example

Original Expansions
   In the centre of the table there stood, **as sentries to a fruit-stand which upheld a pyramid of oranges and American apples**, two squat old-fashioned decanters of cut glass, **one containing port and the other dark sherry**.

   James Joyce, "The Dead"

New Expansions
   On a shelf in the china closet there stood, **like fragile sculptures which boasted an old age and genteel birth**, two squat old-fashioned decanters of cut glass, **one opened, the other unopened**.

---

1. **Now, in the morning air**, her face was still before him.
   Edith Wharton, Ethan Frome

2. Al was out already, **unscrewing the steaming radiator cap with the tips of his fingers, jerking his hand away to escape the spurt when the cap should come loose**.
   John Steinbeck, The Grapes of Wrath

3. With them, **carrying a gnarled walking stick,** was Elmo Goodhue Pipgrass, **the littlest, oldest man I had ever seen**.
   Max Shulman, "The Unlucky Winner"

4. **Later that night, hunched over the kitchen table, still somewhat numbed by the unexpected turn of events,** I chewed thoughtfully on a peanut-butter-and-jelly sandwich, while my mother, **hanging over the sink in her rump-sprung Chinese-red chenille bathrobe,** droned on monotonously.

    Jean Shepherd, "Wanda Hickey's Night of Golden Memories"

5. Their bedroom was on the second floor, **a little cubbyhole really, attained at a special price, its window looking out beyond some rosebushes into the forest, thick with elms and oaks and hedgerows, a brook's rushing waters and bird song waking them in the morning**.

    Oscar Hijuelos, Mr. Ives' Christmas

Practice 2

Expand each sentence at the slash mark (/), using approximately the number of words of the original. Compare yours with the authors' in the References on pages 162–163.

Reduced Sentence

1. She sprang dynamically to her feet, /3, then swiftly and noiselessly crossed over to her bed and, /3, dragged out her suitcase.

    F. Scott Fitzgerald, "Bernice Bobs Her Hair"

2. He stood there, /4, and Rainsford, /6, heard the general's mocking laugh ring through the jungle.

    Richard Connell, "The Most Dangerous Game"

3. /4, he knocked the big man down, and the big man came again, /9.

    Maurice Walsh, "The Quiet Man"

4. We spent several evenings together, and the last one was the funniest, /15.

    Bennett Cerf, At Random

5. That night in the south upstairs chamber, /18, Emmett lay in a kind of trance.

   Jessamyn West, "A Time of Learning"

6. /21, Paul dressed and dashed whistling down the corridor to the elevator.

   Willa Cather, "Paul's Case"

Practice 3

In the last Practice, you were given complete sentences to expand. Now expand incomplete sentences (fragments) by adding a main clause at the slash mark (/), using approximately the number of words of the original. Compare yours with the authors' in the References on page 163.

Sentence Parts

1. /5, helping her get ready, uttering cheerful banalities, and, at the same time, wondering how she felt as she looked in the mirror and saw the partially paralyzed cheek, the deepend lines, the wrinkled skin that hung down from her upper arms.

   Doris Kearns Goodwin, Wait Till Next Year

2. On the outskirts of town, /5, though at first she did not realize it.

   Elizabeth Enright, "Nancy"

3. /6, sweet, hot, and warming his empty stomach.

   Ernest Hemingway, "The Undefeated"

4. When the hostess saw that I was awake and that my safety belt was already fastened, /9, waking the other passengers and asking them to fasten their safety belts.

   Robert Bingham, "The Unpopular Passenger"

5. Running up the street with all his might, /11.

   Murray Heyert, "The New Kid"

6. At night, untired after the day's work, /14.

   Jessamyn West, "A Time of Learning"

Practice 4

For the first four sentences, add one expansion. Compare yours with the originals in the References on pages 163–164. (The original sentences have just one expansion.) For the next four sentences, add two expansions in two different locations. (The original sentences have two expansions.) Punctuate correctly. Compare yours with the originals in the References on page 164.

Add One Expansion

1. In the hall stood an enormous trunk.
   Willa Cather, Youth and the Bright Medusa

2. All members of the staff wore plastic tags bearing their names and color photographs.
   Laurie Colwin, "Animal Behavior"

3. Jerry stood on the landing.
   Joyce Carol Oates, The Wheel of Love and Other Stories

4. They lived in a square two-flat house tightly packed among identical houses in a fog-enveloped street in the Sunset district of San Francisco.
   William Saroyan, "Boy and Girls Together"

Add Two Expansions

5. His teeth were pitifully inadequate by comparison with the mighty fighting fangs of the anthropoids.
   Edgar Rice Burroughs, "Tarzan's First Love"

6. He used to ride,
   Nancy Hale, "The Rider Was Lost"

7. She tossed her book to the deck and hurried to the rail.
   F. Scott Fitzgerald, Flappers and Philosophers

8. It is hardly surprising that so many people lose their tempers with so many other people.
   Shirley Jackson, "About Two Nice People"

Practice 5

Each sentence is a reduced version of a professionally written sentence. You're not told the number, position, or length of the expansions. You must decide all three. After you've finished, compare your sentences with those of the professional authors in the References on page 164.

The only guideline given is the number of words in the original sentence. Try to expand the reduced sentence to approximately the same length.

1. He can feel the eyes on him. (14 words)
    Judith Guest, Original People

2. She made the best meatloaf in the world. (24 words)
    Nancy Friday, My Mother/My Self

3. Weary made Billy take a very close look at his trench knife. (27 words)
    Kurt Vonnegut, Jr., Slaughter-House Five

4. The gardens were laid out so neatly. (28 words)
    Judith Guest, Ordinary People

5. A pale silk scarf is tied around his neck. (29 words)
    Philip Roth, The Professor of Desire

6. The four animals continued to lead their lives. (30 words)
    Kenneth Grahame, The Wind in the Willows

7. He went into the kitchen. (31 words)
    Kurt Vonnegut, Jr., Slaughter-House Five

Practice 6

Select twenty sentences from writing you have done recently. Choose ten of the sentences to expand. For each, add at least one expansion. Vary the lengths, structures, and positions of the expansions.

Focus 5

Reviewing the Techniques

Earlier in this worktext you learned the techniques of unscrambling, imitating, combining, and expanding. Here you will refresh your understanding of those techniques to apply them in the rest of this worktext and in your own writing.

Unscrambling

Practice 1

The sentences below have movable sentence parts that are underlined. Rearrange them in each sentence. Make sure that your rearrangement is as effective as the original.

Example

Original Sentence:
    Tom was on his feet, shouting.
                                    Hal Borland, When the Legends Die

Effective Rearrangements:
    Shouting, Tom was on his feet.

    Tom, shouting, was on his feet.

---

1. Taran cried, his teeth chattering violently.
                                    Lloyd Alexander, The Book of Three

2. The Fog Horn was blowing steadily, once every fifteen seconds.
                                    Ray Bradbury, "The Fog Horn"

3. He sat on a rail fence, watching the night come over Gettysburg.
                                    Michael Shaara, The Killer Angels

4. Slowly, filled with dissatisfaction, he had gone to his room and got into bed.
                                    Betsy Byars, The Summer of the Swans

5. There are boys from broken homes, and boys who have been in difficulty with the law, <u>studying in the classrooms, working in the fields and in the workshops</u>.

   William E. Barrett, The Lilies of the Field

6. Somewhere there, on that desolate plain, was lurking this fiendish man, hiding in a burrow like a wild beast, <u>his heart full of malignancy against the whole race which had cast him out</u>.

   Sir Arthur Conan Doyle, The Hound of the Baskervilles

7. Alan made a business of checking his own reflection in the mirror, <u>giving Norris time to make a clean getaway</u>, while Keeton stood by the door, <u>watching him impatiently</u>.

   Stephen King, Needful Things

8. The garden was <u>to the left of the barn and the pasture</u> hidden from the house by the smokehouse and a pecan grove and a row of little peach trees that <u>because of the drought</u> had dropped hard knotty fruit not even fit to make spiced pickle with.

   Olive Ann Burns, Cold Sassy Tree

9. She ate a great deal and afterward fell asleep herself, and Mary sat and stared at her and watched her fine bonnet slip on one side until she herself fell asleep once more in the corner of the carriage, <u>lulled by the splashing of the rain against the windows</u>.

   Frances Hodgson Burnett, The Secret Garden

10. <u>Standing in front of the room, her blond hair pulled back to emphasize the determination of her face, her body girdled to emphasize the determination of her spine, her eyes holding determinedly to anger</u>, Miss Lass was afraid.

    Rosa Guy, The Friends

*I*mitating

Practice 2

Imitate these model sentences, using your own content but the structure of the model. Imitate one sentence part at a time. Aim for approximating, not duplicating, the model.

Example

Model: Mollie, the foolish, pretty white mare who drew Mr. Jones's trap, came mincing daintily in, chewing a lump of sugar.

        George Orwell, Animal Farm

Sample Student Imitation: The garbage disposal, a noisy, chewing metal mouth that ate the meal's leftovers, began gurgling suddenly then, spitting-up a half-eaten carrot.

---

1. *Model:* Great was his care of them.

      Jack London, "All Gold Cañon"

 Sample Student Imitation: Chilling was her story of anger.

2. *Model:* The big thing, exciting yet frightening, was to talk to her, say what he hoped to do.

      Bernard Malamud, The Assistant

 Sample Student Imitation: An acceptable solution, simple and obvious, is to talk with the manager, emphasize what the workers want to request.

3. *Model:* He had never been hungrier, and he filled his mouth with wine, faintly tarry-tasting from the leather bag, and swallowed.

      Ernest Hemingway, For Whom the Bell Tolls

 Sample Student Imitation: The horse had never been nastier, and it threw its riders to the ground, cold and hard from the frost, and bolted.

4. *Model:* Soon afterwards they retired, Mama in her big oak bed on one side of the room, Emilio and Rosy in their boxes full of straw and sheepskins on the other side of the room.

      John Steinbeck, "Flight"

 Sample Student Imitation: Much later the accountant finished, computer disks in their neat boxes on the right side of the desk, pencils and pens in their containers decorated with seals and designs on the shelf above the desk.

5. *Model:* On stormy nights, when the tide was out, the bay of Fougere, fifty feet below the house, resembled an immense black pit, from which arose mutterings and sighs as if the sands down there had been alive and complaining.

Joseph Conrad, "The Idiots"

Sample Student Imitation: During rush-hour traffic, when his nerves were frazzled, Brent Hammond, a few miles above the speed limit, hit his brakes, from which came sharp peals and leaden grindings as though the metal were alive and hurting.

6. *Model:* The first gray light had just appeared in the living room windows, black mirrors a moment ago, now opening on the view of the woods to the south.

Tracy Kidder, Old Friends

Sample Student Imitation: A great new scent had suddenly caught his attention, a citrus aroma from her perfume, subtly recalling smells of childhood summers in the south of Florida during vacation.

7. *Model:* When I peeped into the sickroom again, Grandpa was bent forward in the rocker, his arms and head resting on the bed by Granny's side.

Olive Ann Burns, Cold Sassy Tree

Sample Student Imitation: When the professor repeated her theory, Toby was leaning forward from his desk, his facial expression and body language fixing on every word of her lecture.

8. *Model:* She was no more than twelve, slender, dirty, nervous and timid as a bird, but beneath the grime as eerily beautiful as a marsh fairy.

Paul Gallico, The Snow Goose

Sample Student Imitation: The rabbit outside was more than vigilant, alert, wary, cautious and watchful as a sentinel, and inside its warren as instinctively maternal as a human mother.

9. *Model:* In the dining hall, over the stone fireplace that was never used, there was a huge stuffed moose head, which looked somehow carnivorous.

Margaret Atwood, "Death by Landscape"

Sample Student Imitation: In his dorm room, on his desk that he shared with his roommate, there was a pile of research notes, which seemed neatly arranged.

10. *Model:* As a girl of ten, Maria had been given a crippled pony, not a true pony, but a small, spotted horse that had injured itself badly on some barbed wire strung by the men who owned the big ranch across the river.

Larry McMurtry, Streets of Laredo

Sample Student Imitation: While an explorer in the damp region, Johnson had gotten a mysterious illness, not a fatal illness, but a rare tropical sickness that had encroached itself selectively on people exposed to a virus that also caused strange diseases of the skin.

Combining

Practice 3

Combine the sets of sentences into just one sentence by making the underlined portions sentence parts of the first sentence. Decide where the sentence parts fit most smoothly into the first sentence. Add commas to punctuate the sentence parts you insert into the first sentence.

Example

Set: The Horned King rode to the wicker baskets and thrust the fire into them. He did this <u>before Gwydion could speak again</u>. The Horned King was <u>bearing a torch</u>.

Combined: Before Gwydion could speak again, the Horned King, bearing a torch, rode to the wicker baskets and thrust the fire into them.

Lloyd Alexander, The Book of Three

---

1. Aunt Dorothy was waiting at the front door with her own small daughter. Aunt Dorothy was <u>tall and bony</u>. Her daughter was <u>Diane</u>.

   Robert Lipsyte, The Contender

2. My mother and father should have stayed in New York. New York was <u>where they met</u>. New York was <u>where they married</u>. New York was <u>where I was born</u>.

   Frank McCourt, Angela's Ashes

3. Craig sat and waited for his father to tell him what he should do next. Craig was <u>calm now, at peace</u>. He sat and waited <u>just as he had done so many times as a child</u>.

   Stephen King, The Langoliers

4. Perhaps an elderly gentleman lived there. He lived there <u>alone</u>. He was <u>someone who had known her grandfather</u>. He was <u>someone who had visited the Parrs in Cummington</u>.

   Joyce Carol Oates, "The Doll" from Haunted

5. The lawyer lay on an old Army cot. The cot was <u>in the closed anteroom</u>. It was one <u>that he kept there for naps</u>. There was <u>a newspaper folded over his face as though he were a corpse being protected from flies</u>.

   Frank Bonham, Chief

*E*xpanding

Practice 4

Expand the sentences at the slash mark, and then check the References on pages 165–166 to see the original sentences.

1. / , a woman sang.

   Ray Bradbury, The Martian Chronicles

2. A large woman, / , got out and waddled over to them.

   Alexander Key, The Forgotten Door

3. Mary asked no more questions but waited in the darkness of her corner, /.

   Frances Hodgson Burnett, The Secret Garden

4. / , he held his temples desperately with both hands and was wretchedly sick.

> *Bill and Vera Cleaver*, Where the Lilies Bloom

5. He walked on, / .

> *Robert Lipsyte*, The Contender

6. / , warriors on high stilts beat upraised swords against their shields.

> *Lloyd Alexander*, The Book of Three

7. Ima Dean, with a huge bag of yellow and red wrapped candies, was sitting on the floor, / , / .

> *Bill and Vera Cleaver*, Where the Lilies Bloom

8. He was a broad, brandy-legged little man with a walrus mustache, with square hands, / and / .

> *John Steinbeck*, The Red Pony

9. They were standing there in front of the locked door in the nearly empty plane, / , when the man in the red shirt and the man in the crew-necked jersey arrived, / .

> *Stephen King*, The Langoliers

10. /, /, /, the boy followed the dog.

> *William Armstrong*, Sounder

2

Using Professional Structures

"The subject, the verb, and the main clause serve merely as the base on which meaning will rise; but the modifier is the essential part of any sentence."

John Erskine

The key to sentence power is knowing and using structures that deepen and enrich meaning. The goal of *Sentence Composing for College* is to teach you the structures that professional writers use in their sentences. The practices in this worktext saturate you with professional models to imitate so you can acquire those structures in your own sentences.

In this part of *Sentence Composing for College*, you will learn, practice, and use three structures that occur with far greater frequency in the writing of professionals than in the writing of students: *absolutes*, *appositives*, *participles*. The goal is for you to become so familiar with those structures that you'll use them with ease and confidence in the sentences you compose.

You'll learn to accessorize your sentences by adding structures professionals use, increasing—just as options raise a car's value—the worth of what you write.

Impact comes from accessories.

Focus 6

Absolute Phrase

Here's a list of sentences, all written by professional writers, but with some parts deleted.

1. She returned to her bench.

2. The boy watched.

3. About the bones, ants were ebbing away.

4. Six boys came over the hill half an hour early that afternoon, running hard.

Now compare the above sentences with the originals. Notice that the part deleted accounts for the distinctiveness of the original sentence. The **boldface** phrases are absolute phrases, one of the sentence parts that differentiates professional writing from student writing. They're frequently used by professional writers but rarely by students. Absolute phrases are an efficient way to combine related ideas in one sentence.

1a. She returned to her bench, **her face showing all the unhappiness that had suddenly overtaken her**.
>   *Theodore Dreiser*, An American Tragedy

2a. The boy watched, **his eyes bulging in the dark**.
>   *Edmund Ware, "An Underground Episode"*

3a. About the bones, ants were ebbing away, **their pincers full of meat**.
>   *Doris Lessing*, African Stories

4a. Six boys came over the hill half an hour early that afternoon, running hard, **their heads down, their forearms working, their breath whistling**.
>   *John Steinbeck*, The Red Pony

Characteristics of Absolute Phrases

An absolute phrase is a modifier that somewhat resembles a complete sentence. Included in every absolute phrase is a subject and a partial verb, which is why it resembles a sentence. However, since the verb is only partial and not complete, absolutes are considered phrases and not clauses. Missing in every absolute phrase is an auxiliary verb—always a form of the verb *to be* (*is*, *are*, *was*, or *were*). Here are examples of absolute phrases with auxiliary verbs inserted (in parentheses) that would change the phrase into a complete sentence. The absolute phrases are taken from the above four sentences.

1a. Her face (was) showing all the happiness that had suddenly overtaken her.

2a. His eyes (were) bulging in the dark.

3a. Their pincers (were) full of meat.

4a. Their heads (were) down. Their forearms (were) working. Their breath (was) whistling.

Another distinguishing characteristic of most absolute phrases is the kind of word they usually begin with. In all of the absolute phrases above, a possessive pronoun is the starting word:

1a. *her*

2a. *his*

3a. *their*

4a. *their*

The class of words called possessive pronouns has only a few members: *my*, *your*, *his*, *her*, *its*, *our*, and *their*. In absolute phrases the possessive pronoun is usually stated, but sometimes it's implied. In the first sentence below, the possessive pronoun that starts the absolute phrase is stated; in the second, it's implied.

Stated

Noiselessly Lenny appeared in the open doorway and stood there looking in, **his** big shoulders nearly filling the opening.

John Steinbeck, Of Mice and Men

Implied

The good dogs came stiffly out of their little house, [**their**] hackles up and deep growls in their throats.

John Steinbeck, The Red Pony

In summary, there are two ways to identify absolute phrases: (1) the phrase **always** can be changed into a sentence by adding an auxiliary verb—usually *was* or *were*—and (2) frequently, **but not always**, the starting word in the absolute phrase is a possessive pronoun, stated or implied.

An absolute phrase can be used as a sentence opener, subject-verb split, or sentence closer.

Sentence Openers

1. **His hands raw**, he reached a flat place at the top.

    Richard Connell, "The Most Dangerous Game"

2. **Each child carrying his little bag of crackling**, we trod the long road home in the cold winter afternoon.

    Peter Abrahams, Tell Freedom

3. Outside, **his carpetbag in his hand**, he stood for a time in the barnyard.

    Jessamyn West, "A Time of Learning"

Subject-Verb Splits

4. Miss Hearne, **her face burning**, hardly listened to these words.

    Brian Moore, The Lonely Passion of Judith Hearne

5. High in the air, a little figure, **his hands thrust in his short jacket pockets,** stood staring out to sea.

    Katherine Mansfield, "The Voyage"

6. An Arab on a motorcycle, **his long robes flying in the wind of his speed**, passed John at such a clip that the spirals of dust from his turnings on the winding road looked like little tornadoes.

Elizabeth Yates, "Standing in Another's Shoes"

Sentence Closers

7. She screamed for Klaus—*shrieked* for him—and Klaus came on the dead run, **his work boots whitened by the half-full pail of milk he had spilled on them**.

Stephen King, "The Two Dead Girls"

8. He walked with a prim strut, swinging out his legs in a half-circle with each step, **his heels biting smartly into the red velvet carpet on the floor**.

Carson McCullers, "The Jockey"

9. Those who had caught sharks had taken them to the shark factory on the other side of the cover where they were hoisted on a block and tackle, **their livers removed, their fins cut off,** and **their hides skinned out,** and **their flesh cut into strips for salting**. (Contains four closers.)

Ernest Hemingway, The Old Man and the Sea

Practice 1

Each of the professionally written sentences below contains an absolute phrase. For each sentence, do the following:

a. Identify the absolute phrase and test your identification by changing the phrase into a complete sentence by adding *was* or *were*.

b. Indicate the possessive pronoun that starts the absolute phrase. Where the pronoun is implied rather than stated, identify the intended pronoun.

c. State the position of the absolute phrase (sentence opener, subject-verb split, sentence closer).

Answers are in the References on page 166.

1. High in the air, a little figure, his hands thrust in his short jacket pockets, stood staring out to sea.

     Katherine Mansfield, "The Voyage"

2. He walked with a prim strut, swinging out his legs in a half-circle with each step, his heels biting smartly into the red velvet carpet on the floor.

     Carson McCullers, "The Jockey"

3. Outside, his carpetbag in his hand, he stood for a time in the barnyard.

     Jessamyn West, "A Time of Learning"

4. Father lay crumped up on the stone floor of the pantry, face down, arms twisted at a curious angle. . . .

     Christy Brown, Down All the Days

Practice 2

Although most absolute phrases begin with possessive pronouns (*my, your, his, her its, our, their*), some do not. Here are examples:

a. He hoisted the sack of feed and took it into the wire dogpen, **the bird dogs crowding around him**, rearing up on him in their eagerness.

     Borden Deal, "The Christmas Hunt"

b. Generally, ships sailed in long convoys, **merchant ship after merchant ship**, like trains of vessels on the water strung out almost as far as the eye could see.

     Edward Rome Snow, "The Light at South Point"

To identify absolute phrases, use the test that applies to every absolute phrase. If you can change it into a sentence by adding *was* or *were*, it's an absolute phrase.

a. The bird dogs [were] crowding around him.

b. Merchant ship [was] after merchant ship.

     Each scrambled sentence below contains an absolute phrase that doesn't begin with a possessive pronoun. Identify the sentence part that is the absolute phrase and then unscramble each sentence to produce the most effective arrangement of the sentence parts. Punctuate correctly. When you finish, compare your sentences with the originals in the References on page 166. Which do you like better? Why?

1a. was awake for quite a long time

 b. the moonlight on her face

 c. thinking about things

 d. I

 e. and watching Catherine sleeping

Ernest Hemingway, A Farewell to Arms

2a. each child carrying his little bag of crackling

 b. we

 c. in the cold winter afternoon

 d. trod the long road home

 e. one of many small groups of children

Peter Abrahams, Tell Freedom

3a. I

 b. each set upon a carved wooden base

 c. looked across to a lighted case of Chinese design

 d. which held delicate-looking statues

 e. of horses and birds, small vases and bowls

Ralph Ellison, Invisible Man

Practice 3

Each scrambled sentence contains more than one absolute phrase. Unscramble each sentence to produce the most effective arrangement of the sentence parts. Punctuate correctly. When you finish, compare your sentences with the originals in the References on pages 166–167. Which do you like better? Why?

1a. while Buck struggled in fury

  b. then the rope tightened mercilessly

  c. and his great chest panting

  d. his tongue lolling out of his mouth

Jack London, The Call of the Wild

2a. her shoulders drooping a little

  b. her glasses winking in the sunlight

  c. she was now standing arms akimbo

  d. her head cocked to one side

Harper Lee, To Kill a Mockingbird

3a. wherever it settled its weight

  b. it ran

  c. its taloned feet clawing damp earth

  d. leaving prints six inches deep

  e. its pelvic bones crushing aside trees and bushes

Ray Bradbury, "A Sound of Thunder"

4a. as if he could squeal or laugh out loud

  b. and then

  c. his hand in one pocket clutching the money

  d. he felt

  e. his feet sinking in the soft nap of the carpet

Theodore Dreiser, An American Tragedy

5a. within you could hear the sighs and murmurs as the furthest chambers of it died

  b. closing up forever

  c. the organs malfunctioning

  d. everything shutting off

  e. liquids running a final instant from pocket to sac to spleen

Ray Bradbury, "A Sound of Thunder"

Practice 4

Underneath the model sentence are two imitations. The model and the imitations contain absolute phrases. The imitations are presented as a list of scrambled sentence parts for you to unscramble to duplicate the structure of the model. Unscramble each of the two sentences to produce a sentence similar in structure to the model. Identify the absolute phrases in the model and the two imitations. Compare your sentences with the ones in the References on page 167.

> Model: The motorcycle on the sidewalk speeded up and skidded obliquely into a plate-glass window, the front wheel bucking and climbing the brick base beneath the window.
> *Frank Rooney, "Cyclist's Raid"*

Scrambled Imitations

1a. the other customers rallying and demanding the same reduction in the cost

b. one customer in the line spoke out

c. about the unfair price

d. and ranted continuously

2a. and moved quickly

b. one couple heading and leading the rest through the complicated steps

c. into two lines

d. several dancers near the band joined together

Practice 5

Read the model and then the list of sentences underneath it. Combine the list into one sentence having basically the same structure as the model. Compare your sentence with the ones in the References on page 167. Finally, write an imitation of the model with the same structure but your own content.

Example

Model: He returned, shuddering, five minutes later, **his arms soaked and red to the elbows**.

Ray Bradbury, "A Sound of Thunder"

Sentences to Be Combined

a. This is about the soldiers.

b. They retreated.

c. They were shivering.

d. This happened two days ago.

e. Their spirits were outraged.

f. In addition, their spirits were crushed.

g. This effect on their spirits was caused by the defeat.

Combination

The soldiers retreated, shivering, two days ago, **their spirits outraged and crushed by the defeat**.

Imitation

She left, smiling, a minute before, **her Andrew Wyeth print matted and framed in green**.

---

1. Model: The electric train was there waiting, **all the lights on**.
   Ernest Hemingway, A Farewell to Arms

   a. The youngest brother was nearby.

   b. He was resting.

   c. All his work was over.

2. Model: As soon as she was well, we went to Southend-on-the-Sea for a holiday, **Mother outfitting us completely with new clothes**.
   Charlie Chaplin, My Autobiography

   a. It happened as soon as it was over.

   b. What happened then was that they pranced around Gracie.

c. They did their prancing like courtiers.

d. Paul was wooing her disgustingly.

e. He wooed her with his stretched smiles.

3. Model: Then, very afraid, she shook her head warningly, and touched a finger to her lips and shook her head again, **her eyes pleading with him**.
    James Clavell, Shogun

a. Later, he was very happy.

b. He held the baby.

c. He held it soothingly.

d. In addition, he brought the music box to her.

e. He wound the toy up.

f. His voice was singing with it.

4. Model: The old woman pointed upwards interrogatively and, on my aunt's nodding, proceeded to toil up the narrow staircase before us, **her bowed head being scarcely above the level of the banister-rail**.
    James Joyce, "The Sisters"

a. The student teacher erased everything quickly.

b. In addition, she did something with a hurried cover-up.

c. She started to call out the spelling words.

d. She did this for us.

e. Her embarrassment was coming from something.

f. It was coming from her misspelling.

g. The misspelling was on the chalkboard.

Practice 6

Write an imitation of each of the models.

Sentence Openers

1. Outside, **his carpetbag in his hand**, he stood for a time in the barnyard.

   Jessamyn West, *"A Time of Learning"*

2. **His head aching, his throat sore**, he forgot to light the cigarette.

   Sinclair Lewis, Cass Timberlane

3. A moment later, **his hands upraised, his pony's bridle reins caught in the crook of one arm**, a young man moved into the zone of light that shone bravely out through Tim Geogehan's back window.

   F. R. Buckley, *"Gold-Mounted Guns"*

Subject-Verb Splits

4. A seared man, **his charred clothes fuming where the blast had blown out the fire**, rose from the curb.

   Fritz Leiber, *"A Bad Day for Sales"*

5. Some got out, **their bodies burnt and flattened**, and went off not knowing where they were going.

   Ernest Hemingway, A Farewell to Arms

6. Mammoth Mister Victor Mature, **sweat streaming down his face**, met and held the lion, bigger now as the close-up showed its mammoth jaws, its mammoth fangs.

   Brian Moore, The Lonely Passion of Judith Hearne

Sentence Closers

7. A water snake slipped along on the pool, **its head held up like a little periscope**.

   John Steinbeck, Of Mice and Men

8. Jack stood up as he said this, **the bloodied knife in his hands**.

   William Golding, Lord of the Flies

9. My brother came to my side, **his eyes drawn by the blazing straws**.

   Richard Wright, Native Son

Practice 7

In the first sentence in each group, a slash mark (/) indicates that the original sentence has an absolute phrase at that place. Combine the rest of the sentences into an absolute phrase that will fit smoothly into that place. Compare your results with the originals in the References on pages 167–168. Write an imitation of the resulting sentences, using your own content but the structure of the model.

Example

   a. She slid back the roof of the cockpit once again, / .

   b. Her nose was wrinkling.

   c. It was wrinkling at the rankness of the morass.

   d. The morass was dripping.

   e. The morass was encircling them.

Combination with Absolute Phrase

She slid back the roof of the cockpit once again, **her nose wrinkling at the rankness of the dripping morass encircling them**.

               Alan Dean Foster, "Splinter of the Mind's Eye"

Imitation

He climbed down the limb of the cherry tree very slowly, **his arms tightening around the bark of the big branch supporting him**.

1a. The town lay on a broad estuary, / .

  b. The town's old yellow plastered buildings were hugging something.

  c. The buildings were hugging the beach.

               From *John Steinbeck*, The Pearl

2a. Like giants they toiled, / .

  b. The days were flashing on the heels of days like dreams.

c. This happened as they heaped the treasure up.
    From Jack London, The Call of the Wild

3a. An Arab on a motorcycle, / , passed John at such a clip that the spirals of dust from his turnings on the winding road looked like little tornadoes.

b. His robes were flying.

c. The robes were long.

d. The robes were flying in the wind.

e. The wind was of his speed.
    From Elizabeth Yates,
    "Standing in Another's Shoes"

4a. In solid phalanxes the leaders crowded about the three jaguars, /, / . (two absolute phrases)

b. Their tusks were thrust.

c. The thrusting was forward.

d. Their little eyes were bloodshot with anger.

e. In addition, they were bloodshot with battle lust.
    From Tom Gill, "Jungle War"

Practice 8

Combine each list of sentences into one sentence containing an absolute phrase. Underline each phrase. You may eliminate words and change their form as long as the intended meaning remains. Punctuate correctly. When you finish, compare your sentences with the originals in the References on page 168.

1a. I could hear him.

b. He was crashing down the hill.

c. He was crashing toward the sea.

d. The frightening laughter was echoing back.
    From Theodore Taylor, The Cay

2a. Finny and I went along the Boardwalk.

b. We were in our sneakers and white slacks.

c. Finny was in a light blue polo shirt.

d. I was in a T-shirt.

From *John Knowles*, A Separate Peace

3a. It happened all the time he was reading the newspaper.

b. What happened was that his wife leaned out of the window.

c. His wife was a fat woman with a white face.

d. She was gazing into the street.

e. Her thick white arms were folded under her loose breast on the window sill.

From *Bernard Malamud*,
"A Summer's Reading"

4a. To the right of them the gym meditated.

b. It meditated behind its gray walls.

c. The windows were shining back at the sun.

d. The windows were high.

e. The windows were wide.

f. The windows were oval-topped.

From *John Knowles*, A Separate Peace

Practice 9

Expand the sentences by adding approximately the same number of words the authors used for their absolute phrases. The number is next to the slash mark (/). To help you start, the beginning words of the absolute phrases are provided in **boldface**. Compare your absolute phrases with the originals in the References on pages 168–169.

1. Now, in the waning daylight, he turned into Glover Street toward his home, /10 **his arms.** . . .

Norman Katkov "The Torn Invitation"

2. As they drove off, Wilson saw her standing under the big tree, looking pretty rather than beautiful in her faintly rosy khaki, /17 **her dark hair** . . . , /12 **her face.** . . .

   Ernest Hemingway,
   "The Short Happy Life of Francis Macomber"

3. His great chest was low to the ground, /5 **his head** . . . , /5 **his feet.** . . , /10 **the claws.** . . .

   Jack London, The Call of the Wild

4. In front of the house where we lived, the mountain went down steeply to the little plain along the lake, and we sat on the porch of the house in the sun and saw the winding of the road down the mountain-side and the terraced vineyards on the side of the lower mountain, /8 **the vines** . . . and /6 **the fields** . . . , and below the vineyards, /13 **the houses.** . . .

   Ernest Hemingway, A Farewell to Arms

Practice 10

Add an absolute phrase to each of the reduced sentences below, blending your content with the rest of the sentence. Each of the sentences in its original, complete version had an absolute phrase in the place indicated by the slash mark (/). Compare your sentences with the originals in the References on page 169.

1. He began scrambling up the wooden pegs nailed to the side of the tree, / .

   John Knowles, A Separate Peace

2. Touser roused himself under Fowler's desk and scratched another flea, / .

   Clifford D. Simak, "Desertion"

3. They were smiling, / , / .

   Jack Finney, "Of Missing Persons"

4. Wearing an Indian dhoti, / , bald, slight, with a bony face, deep-set eyes the size of peas, / , / , he sat on a hard wooden chair, at center stage, tucking his legs under him in a yogic manner.

   Oscar Hijuelos, Mr. Ives' Christmas

*F*ocus 7

Appositive Phrase

Here's a list of sentences, all written by professional writers, but with some parts deleted.

1. It went away slowly.

2. The land that lay stretched out before him became of vast significance.

3. However, I looked with a mixture of admiration and awe at Peter.

4. That night in the south upstairs chamber Emmett lay in a kind of trance.

Now compare the above sentences with the originals. Notice that the parts deleted account for the distinctiveness of the original sentences. The **boldface** phrases are appositives, another of the sentence parts that differentiate professional writing from student writing. They're frequently used by professional writers but rarely by students. Appositive phrases are an efficient way to combine related ideas in one sentence.

1a.   It went away slowly, **the feeling of disappointment that came sharply after the thrill that made his shoulders ache**.

Ernest Hemingway, "Big Two-Hearted River: Part II"

2a.   The land that lay stretched out before him became of vast significance, **a place peopled by his fancy with a new race of men sprung from himself**.

Sherwood Anderson, Winesburg, Ohio

3a.   However, I looked with a mixture of admiration and awe at Peter, **a boy who could and did imitate a police siren every morning on his way to the showers**.

Robert Russell, To Catch an Angel

4a.   That night in the south upstairs chamber, **a hot little room where a full-leafed chinaberry tree shut all the air from the single window**, Emmett lay in a kind of trance.

Jessamyn West, "A Time of Learning"

Characteristics of Appositive Phrases

An appositive is a noun that identifies an adjacent noun or pronoun. An appositive phrase is the appositive noun plus any of its modifiers. Here are examples. The complete appositive phrase is in **boldface**.

1. Poppa, **a good quiet man**, spent the last hours before our parting moving aimlessly about the yard, keeping to himself and avoiding me.

    Gordon Parks, "My Mother's Dream for Me"

2. The boy looked at them, **big black ugly insects**.

    Doris Lessing, African Stories

3. Hour after hour he stood there, silent, motionless, **a shadow carved in ebony and moonlight**.

    James V. Marshall, Walkabout

4. A man, **a weary old pensioner with a bald dirty head and a stained brown corduroy waistcoat**, appeared at the door of a small gate lodge.

    Brian Moore, The Lonely Passion of Judith Hearne

5. He had the appearance of a man who had done a great thing, **something greater than any ordinary man would do**.

    John Henrik Clarke, "The Boy Who Painted Christ Black"

An appositive phrase can be used as a sentence opener, subject-verb split, or sentence closer.

Sentence Openers

1. **One of eleven brothers and sisters**, Harriet was a moody, willful child.

    Langston Hughes, "Road to Freedom"

2. **A balding, smooth-faced man**, he could have been anywhere between forty and sixty.

   Harper Lee, To Kill a Mockingbird

3. **A short, round boy of seven**, he took little interest in troublesome things, preferring to remain on good terms with everyone.

   Mildred D. Taylor, Roll of Thunder, Hear My Cry

Subject-Verb Splits

4. Visitors, **friends of her parents or little girls her own age**, were always astonished when they first saw it.

   Joyce Carol Oates, "The Doll" from Haunted

5. The Union commander, **a tall blond sunburned man named John Buford**, rode up the long slope to the top of the hill, into the cemetery.

   Michael Shaara, The Killer Angels

6. Van'ka Zhukov, **a boy of nine who had been apprenticed to the shoemaker Alyakhin three months ago**, was staying up that Christmas eve.

   Anton Chekhov, "Van'ka"

Sentence Closers

7. There was a sizable number of well-read inmates, **especially the popular debaters**.

   Malcolm X, (with Alex Haley)
   The Autobiography of Malcolm X

8. Lamp Trimmer Samuel Hemming, lying in his bunk, heard a curious hissing sound coming from the forepeak, **the compartment closest to the bow of the *Titanic***.

   Walter Lord, A Night to Remember

9. Ives and Ramirez parked, and upon approaching the entranceway saw Father Jimenez, **an old man now in wire-rim glasses peering out from behind the screen**.

   Oscar Hijuelos, Mr. Ives' Christmas

Practice 1

Each of the professionally written sentences below contains an appositive phrase. For each sentence, do the following:

a. Identify the appositive phrase.

b. Name the word the appositive phrase identifies.

c. State the position of the appositive phrase (sentence opener, subject-verb split, sentence closer).

Answers are in the References on page 169.

1. The writer, an old man with a white mustache, had some difficulty in getting into bed.
   Sherwood Anderson, Winesburg, Ohio

2. Halfway there he heard the sound he dreaded, the hollow, rasping cough of a horse.
   John Steinbeck, The Red Pony

3. Mr. Mick Malloy, cashier at the Ulster and Connaught Bank, draped his grey sports jacket neatly on a hanger and put on his black shantung work coat.
   Brian Moore, The Lonely Passion of Judith Hearne

4. A self-educated man, he had accepted the necessary smattering of facts of science and a serene indulgence, as simply so much further proof of what the Creator could do when He put His hand to it.
   Wilbur Daniel Steele, "The Man Who Saw Through Heaven"

Practice 2

Identify the sentence part that is the appositive phrase and next unscramble each sentence to produce the most effective arrangement of the sentence parts. When you finish, compare your sentences with the originals in the References on page 170. Which do you like better? Why?

1a. struggled as usual

 b. she

 c. to maintain her calm, composed, friendly bearing

d. a sort of mask she wore all over her body

D. H. Lawrence, "The Blind Man"

2a. an old, bowlegged fellow in a pale-blue sweater

b. the judge

c. and was reading over some notes he had taken

d. had stopped examining the animals

e. on the back of a dirty envelope

Jessamyn West, "The Lesson"

3a. of a small gate lodge

b. appeared

c. a weary old pensioner with a bald dirty head and a stained brown corduroy waistcoat

d. a man

e. at the door

Brian Moore, The Lonely Passion of Judith Hearne

Practice 3

Each scrambled sentence below contains more than one appositive phrase. Unscramble each sentence to produce the most effective arrangement of the sentence parts. Punctuate correctly. When you finish, compare your sentences with the originals in the References on page 170. Which do you like better? Why?

1a. talked continually of virginity

b. the son of a jeweler in Winesburg

c. one of them

d. a slender young man with white hands

Sherwood Anderson, Winesburg, Ohio

2a. went over to Tom Willy's saloon

b. in the late afternoon

    c.   Will Henderson

    d.   and editor of the *Eagle*

    e.   owner

                                     Sherwood Anderson, Winesburg, Ohio

3a. and the jingle of trace chains

    b.   was louder

    c.   drag of brakes

    d.   the sound of the approaching grain teams

    e.   thud of big hooves on hard ground.

                                    John Steinbeck, Of Mice and Men

4a. with the butt of a teamster's whip

    b.   once Enoch Bentley

    c.   old Tom Bentley

    d.   struck his father

    e.   and the old man seemed likely to die

    f.   the older one of the boys

                                    Sherwood Anderson, Winesburg, Ohio

5a. with devil-may-care eyes and a long humorous nose

    b.   Mr. Mick Malloy

    c.   tall cashier with a dignified face

    d.   a nice sort of fellow

    e.   tall, young secret gambler

    f.   a gentlemanly bank clerk

    g.   became Mr. Malloy

                                    Brian Moore, The Lonely Passion of Judith Hearne

Practice 4

Underneath the model sentence are two imitations. The model and the imitations contain appositive phrases. The imitations are presented as a list of scrambled sentence parts for you to unscramble to duplicate the structure of the model. Unscramble each of the two sentences to produce a sentence similar in structure to the model. Identify the appositive phrases in the model and the two imitations. Compare your sentences with the ones in the References on page 170.

> Model: Beside the fireplace old Doctor Winter sat, bearded and simple and benign, **historian and physician to the town**.
>
> *John Steinbeck*, The Moon Is Down

Scrambled Imitations

1a.   president and valedictorian of the senior class

b.   by the podium

c.   intelligent and composed and smiling

d.   scholarly Henrietta stood

2a.   beaming and affectionate and happy

b.   bride and groom in their finery

c.   they danced

d.   under the canopy

Practice 5

Read the model and then the list of sentences underneath it. Combine the list into one sentence having basically the same structure as the model. The order in which the sentences are listed is the order of the sentence parts of the model. In other words, convert the first sentence into the first sentence part of the model, the second sentence into the second part, and so forth. Compare yours with the ones in the References on pages 170–171. Finally, write an imitation of the model, with the same structure but your own content.

Example

> Model: Mr. Cattanzara, **a stocky, bald-headed man who worked in a change booth on an IRT station**, lived on the next block after George's, above a shoe repair store.
>
> *Bernard Malamud, "A Summer's Reading"*

Sentences to Be Combined

a. This is about Jan Carter.

b. She is an unabashed, sun-tanned flirt.

c. She had smiled at him in the cafeteria line.

d. She transferred to the department near Tom's.

e. She transferred for a "chance" meeting.

Combination

Jan Carter, **an unabashed, sun-tanned flirt who had smiled at him in the cafeteria line**, transferred to the department near Tom's, for a "chance" meeting.

Imitation

Tom Zengler, **the slower, more heavy-handed pianist who had studied under Professor Samione for a decade**, performed in the recital hall near Jacob's, with an obvious competitive attitude.

---

1. Model: Among the company was a lawyer, **a young man of about twenty-five**.

   Anton Chekhov, "The Bet"

   a. She was near the statue.

   b. She was an obvious tourist.

   c. She was an older lady.

   d. She had a Kodak camera.

2. Model: Sady Ellison, **the daughter of Long Butt Ellison**, worked as a waitress for Turkey Plott in a defiant and condescending fashion.

   Wayne Kernodle, "Last of the Rugged Individualists"

   a. This is about *Gone with the Wind*.

   b. That is the movie with the most re-issues.

   c. It originated as a novel.

   d. The novel was of the old South.

e. The novel was by someone who was unglamorous.

f. The someone was also unknown.

g. The someone was an authoress.

3. Model: Captain Bentick was a family man, **a lover of dogs and pink children and Christmas**.

> *John Steinbeck*, The Moon Is Down

a. "Missouri" is a casserole.

b. The casserole is special.

c. It is a blend of several ingredients.

d. It has potatoes.

e. It has tomatoes.

f. The tomatoes are stewed.

g. It has hamburger.

4. Model: He was close to twenty and had needs with the neighborhood girls, but no money to spend, and he couldn't get more than an occasional few cents because his father was poor, and his sister Sophie, who resembled George, **a tall, bony girl of twenty-three**, earned very little, and what she had she kept for herself.

> *Bernard Malamud, "A Summer's Reading"*

a. We were far from our destination.

b. In addition, we were making good time on the interstate.

c. But there was no time to squander.

d. In addition, Dad wouldn't stop more than twice a day.

e. Although we kids were itchy, he wouldn't stop.

f. In addition, Mom was the one who kept the peace.

g. She was a shrewd, gentle arbitrator.

h. She had Solomon's mind.

i. She circumvented some flare-ups.

j. And she did something with those she couldn't circumvent.

k. She left those to Heaven.

Practice 6

Write an imitation of each of the models.

Sentence Openers

1. **One of eleven brothers and sisters**, Harriet was a moody, willful child.

    Langston Hughes, "Road to Freedom"

2. **A self-educated man**, he had accepted the necessary smattering of facts of science with a serene indulgence, as simply so much further proof of what the Creator could do when He put His hand to it.

    Wilbur Daniel Steele, "The Man Who Saw Through Heaven"

Subject-Verb Splits

3. One of these, **a young woman who turned to look**, called to Yakov, but by then the wagon was out of the marketplace, scattering some chickens nesting in the ruts of the road and a flock of jabbering ducks, as it clattered on.

    Bernard Malamud, The Fixer

4. Henry Strader, **an old man who had been on the farm since Jesse came into possession and who before David's time had never been known to make a joke**, made the same joke every morning.

    Sherwood Anderson, Winesburg, Ohio

Sentence Closers

5. In all the years which have since elapsed, she remains the woman I loved and lost, **the unattainable one**.

    Henry Miller, Stand Still Like the Hummingbird

6. It had a black spot on it, **the black spot Mr. Summer had made the night before with the heavy pencil in the coal-company office**.

    Shirley Jackson, "The Lottery"

Practice 7

In the first sentence in each group, a slash mark (/) indicates that the original sentence has an appositive phrase at that place. Combine the sentences underneath into an appositive phrase that will fit smoothly into that place. Compare your results with the originals in the References on page 171. Write an imitation of the resulting sentence, using your own content but the structure of the model.

Example

a. She was playing the Canteen at Aldershot at the time, /.

b. The theatre was grubby.

c. The theatre was mean.

d. The theatre was catering mostly to soldiers.

Combination with Appositive Phrase

> She was playing the Canteen at the Aldershot at the time, **a grubby, mean theatre catering mostly to soldiers**.
>
> *Charlie Chaplin*, My Autobiography

Imitation

> He was inspecting a condemned school near Thorn Road around noon, **an old, stone building closing probably in June**.

1a. On this Sunday morning the postman and the policeman had gone fishing in the boat of Mr. Corell, / .

b. Mr. Corell was the storekeeper.

c. He was popular.

> From *John Steinbeck*, The Moon Is Down

2a. The real estate agent, / , soon joined them.

b. The agent was a man.

    c.   He was old.

    d.   He was a man with a smiling face.

    e.   The face was hypocritical.
> From *Willa Cather, "The Sculptor's Funeral"*

3a.   They approached the domed synagogue with its iron weathercock, / , for the time being resting in peace.

    b.   The synagogue was a yellow-walled building.

    c.   It was pock-marked.

    d.   It was a building with a door.

    e.   The door was oak.
> From *Bernard Malamud*, The Fixer

4a.   Lieutenant Tonder was a poet, / .

    b.   He was a bitter poet.

    c.   He was a poet who dreamed of perfect, ideal love.

    d.   The love was of elevated young men for girls.

    e.   The girls were poor.
> From *John Steinbeck*, The Moon Is Down

Practice 8

Combine each list of sentences into one sentence containing an appositive phrase. Underline each phrase. You may eliminate words and change their form as long as the intended meaning remains. Punctuate correctly. When you finish, compare your sentences with the originals in the References on page 171.

1a.   Something happens at the gate.

    b.   There, I show the pass to a private.

    c.   The private is young.

    d.   The private is Japanese.

e. The private is the sentry.

From *Richard E. Kim*, Lost Names

2a. It happened when he was twelve.

b. Then, his mother married an executive.

c. The executive was of a machine tool company.

d. The company was in Cleveland.

e. The executive was an engineer.

f. He was an engineer who had adult children of his own.

From *Glendon Swarthout,*
Bless the Beasts and Children

3a. My patient was a woman.

b. She was modern.

c. She was intelligent.

d. She with her five children seemed trapped.

e. She seemed as trapped as her forebears.

f. Her forebears were in Victorian times.

g. In Victorian times was before the emancipation of women.

From *Rollo May*, Love and Will

4a. On the bark of the tree was scored something.

b. What was scored there was a name.

c. The name was of Deacon Peabody.

d. Deacon Peabody was a man.

e. He was eminent.

f. It was he who had waxed wealthy.

g. He did this by driving bargains.

h. The bargains were shrewd.

i. The bargains were with the Indians.

From *Washington Irving,*
"The Devil and Tom Walker"

Practice 9

Expand the sentences by adding approximately the same number of words the authors used for their appositive phrases. The number is next to the slash mark (/). To help you start, the beginning words of the appositive phrases are provided in **boldface**. Compare your appositive phrases with the originals in the References on page 172.

1. Thus, one noontime, coming back from the office lunch downstairs a little earlier than usual, he found her and several of the foreign-family girls, as well as four of the American girls, surrounding Polish Mary, / 10 **one of the** . . . , who was explaining in rather a high key how a certain "feller" whom she had met the night before had given her a beaded bag, and for what purpose.
   Theodore Dreiser, An American Tragedy

2. The rest were standing around in hatless, smoky little groups of twos and threes and fours inside the heated waiting room, talking in voices that, almost without exception, sounded collegiately dogmatic, as though each young man, in his strident, conversational turn, was clearing up, once and for all, some highly controversial issue, /14 **one that.** . . .
   J. D. Salinger, Franny and Zooey

3. Out in the distance the fans of windmills twinkled, turning, and about the base of each, about the drink tank, was a speckle of dark dots, /17 **a herd of cattle.** . . .
   Glendon Swarthout, Bless the Beasts and Children

4. Perhaps two or three times a year we would come together at a party, one of those teen-age affairs which last until dawn with singing and dancing and silly games such as "Kiss the Pillow," or "Post Office," /21 **the game which.** . . .
   Henry Miller, Stand Still Like the Hummingbird

Practice 10

Add an appositive phrase to each of the reduced sentences below, blending your content with the rest of the sentence. Each of the sentences in its original, complete version had an appositive phrase in the place indicated by the slash mark. Compare your sentences with the originals in the References on pages 172–173.

1. My bed was an army cot, / .
   James Thurber, "The Night the Bed Fell"

2. He, / , had fled because of superior perceptions and knowledge.
   Stephen Crane, The Red Badge of Courage

3. I had hardly any patience with the serious work of life which, now that it stood between me and desire, seemed to me child's play, / .
   James Joyce, "Araby"

4. There was Major Hunter, / , / . (two appositive phrases)
   John Steinbeck, The Moon Is Down

*F*ocus 8

Participial Phrase

*I*dentifying the Participial Phrase

Here's a list of sentences, all written by professional writers, but with some parts deleted.

1. We could see the lake and the mountains across the lake on the French side.

2. Sadao had his reward.

3. The sun rose clear and bright.

4. Spencer took half an hour.

Now compare the above sentences with the originals. Notice that the part deleted accounts for the distinctiveness of the original sentence. The **boldface** phrases are participles, one of the sentence parts that appears frequently in professional writing, but rarely in student writing. Participle phrases are an efficient way to combine related ideas into one sentence.

1a. **Sitting up in bed eating breakfast**, we could see the lake and the mountains across the lake on the French side.

   Ernest Hemingway, A Farewell to Arms

2a. Sadao, **searching the spot of black in the twilight sea that night**, had his reward.

   Pearl S. Buck, "The Enemy"

3a. The sun rose clear and bright, **tinging the foamy crests of the waves with a reddish purple**.

   Alexander Dumas, Count of Monte Cristo

4a. Spencer took half an hour, **swimming in one of the pools which was filled with the seasonal rain, waiting for the pursuers to catch up to him**.

> *Ray Bradbury*, The Martian Chronicles

Earlier in this worktext, you studied two other structures (absolute phrases and appositive phrases) that are used frequently by professionals but infrequently by students. Even though those two structures are quite common in professional writing, participial phrases are the most common, occurring so frequently that you can find examples on almost any page of a book.

Characteristics of Participial Phrases

A participial phrase describes a noun or pronoun. The first word in the phrase is almost always the participle itself. There are two types of participles. Present participles always end in *ing*. Past participles usually end in either *ed* or *en*. Below in **boldface** are examples.

Present Participles

1. She was quite far from the windows which were to her left, and behind her were a couple of tall bookcases, **containing all the books of the factory library**.

> *John Hersey*, Hiroshima

2. Minute fungi overspread the whole exterior, **hanging in a fine tangled web-work from the eaves**.

> *Edgar Allan Poe, "The Fall of the House of Usher"*

3. **Standing there in the middle of the street**, Marty suddenly thought of Halloween, of the winter and snowballs, of the schoolyard.

> *Murray Heyert, "The New Kid"*

4. Professor Kazan, **wearing a spotlessly white tropical suit and a wide-brimmed hat**, was the first ashore.

> *Arthur C. Clarke*, Dolphin Island

5. He walked to the corner of the lot, then back again, **studying the simple terrain as if deciding how best to effect an entry, frowning** and **scratching his head**.

     Harper Lee, To Kill a Mockingbird

Past Participles

6. In six months a dozen small towns had been laid down upon the naked planet, **filled with sizzling neon tubes and yellow electric bulbs**.

     Ray Bradbury, The Martian Chronicles

7. The tent, **illumined by candle**, glowed warmly in the midst of the plain.

     Jack London, The Call of the Wild

8. **Enchanted** and **enthralled**, I stopped her constantly for details.

     Richard Wright, Black Boy

9. The other shoji slammed open, and **unseen**, Buntaro stamped away, **followed by the guard**.

     James Clavell, Shogun

10. Her hair, **braided** and **wrapped around her head**, made an ash-blonde crown.

     John Steinbeck, The Grapes of Wrath

A participial phrase can be used as a sentence opener, subject-verb split, or sentence closer.

Sentence Openers

1. **Whistling**, he let the escalator waft him into the still night air.

     Ray Bradbury, Fahrenheit 451

2. **Looking over their own troops**, they saw mixed masses slowly getting into regular form.

     Stephen Crane, The Red Badge of Courage

3. **Amazed at the simplicity of it all**, I understood everything as never before.

     Alphonse Daudet, "The Last Lesson"

Subject-Verb Splits

4. My father, **cautioning me not to work a horse till he had fed fully**, said I had plenty of time to eat myself.

   Lincoln Steffens, "A Boy on Horseback"

5. Eckels, **balanced on the narrow path**, aimed his rifle playfully.

   Ray Bradbury, "A Sound of Thunder"

6. The sight of Mick's exploring beam of light, **flashing and flickering through the submarine darkness a few yards away**, reminded him that he was not alone.

   Arthur C. Clarke, Dolphin Island

Sentence Closers

7. The entire crowd in the saloon gathered about me now, **urging me to drink**.

   Richard Wright, Black Boy

8. She called to him, **excited**.

   Daphne du Maurier, "The Birds"

9. The magician patted the hand, **holding it quietly with a thumb on its blue veins, waiting for life to revive**. (two participial phrases)

   T. S. White, Book of Merlyn

Practice 1

Each of the professionally written sentences below contains a participial phrase. For each sentence, do the following:

a. Identify the participial phrase and indicate the type of participle (present or past).

b. Name the word that the participial phrase describes.

c. State the position of the phrase (sentence opener, subject-verb split, or sentence closer).

Answers are in the References on page 173.

1. Manuel, lying on the ground, kicked at the bull's muzzle with his slippered feet.

   Ernest Hemingway, "The Undefeated"

2. Clutching the clawing kitten to her collarbone, her hair in her open mouth, she bawled encouragement to them.

   Elizabeth Enright, "Nancy"

3. They were diggers in clay, transformed by lantern light into a race of giants.

   Edmund Ware, "An Underground Episode"

4. Ruthie, dressed in a real dress of pink muslin that came below her knees, was a little serious in her young-ladyness.

   John Steinbeck, The Grapes of Wrath

Practice 2

Unscramble each list of sentence parts three times: first, to produce a sentence with a participial phrase in the sentence opener position; next, in the subject-verb split position; and finally, in the sentence closer position. Classify the use of each position as either acceptable or unacceptable. Tell which position you prefer. Compare your sentences with the originals in the References on page 173.

1a. was waiting on the landing outside

  b. Bernard

  c. wearing a black turtleneck sweater, dirty flannels, and slippers.

   Brian Moore, The Lonely Passion of Judith Hearne

2a. could see the lake

  b. sitting up in bed eating breakfast

  c. we

  d. and the mountains across the lake on the French side

   Ernest Hemingway, A Farewell to Arms

3a. coming down the pole

  b. with no control over my movements

  c. had a sense

  d. I

  e. of being whirled violently through the air.

Richard E. Byrd, Alone

4a. black

  b. a little house

  c. perched on high piles

  d. in the distance

  e. appeared

Joseph Conrad, "The Lagoon"

5a. screaming and begging to be allowed to go with her mother

  b. when we had made our way downstairs

  c. saw the woman with the lovely complexion

  d. Miss Pilzer

  e. we

Gerda Weissmann Klein, All But My Life

Practice 3

Each scrambled sentence below contains more than one participial phrase. Unscramble each to produce the most effective arrangement of the sentence parts. When you finish, compare your sentences with the originals in the References on page 174.

1a. with the cautious, half-furtive effort of the sightless

  b. and thumping his way before him

  c. he was a blind beggar

  d. carrying the traditional battered cane

MacKinlay Kantor, "A Man Who Had No Eyes"

2a.   all had the look of invalids crawling into the hospital on their last legs

 b.   the passengers

 c.   blinking their eyes against the blinding sunlight

 d.   emerging from the mildewed dimness of the customs shed
                    Katherine Anne Porter, Ship of Fools

3a.   and yet knowing no way to avoid it

 b.   that winter my mother and brother came

 c.   buying furniture on the installment plan

 d.   and we set up housekeeping

 e.   being cheated
                              Richard Wright, Black Boy

4a.· where George Willard sat listening

 b.   and breaking off the tale

 c.   Doctor Parcival

 d.   in the office of the *Winesburg Eagle*

 e.   jumping to his feet

 f.   began to walk up and down
                    Sherwood Anderson, Winesburg, Ohio

5a.   came up slowly

 b.   his long embroidered robe streaming over her arm almost to the ground

 c.   a young Mexican woman

 d.   dressed in the elegant, perpetual mourning of her caste

 e.   who carried her baby

 f.   softened and dispirited by recent childbirth

 g.   leaning on the arm of the Indian nurse
                    Katherine Anne Porter, Ship of Fools

Practice 4

Underneath the model sentence are two imitations. The model and the imitations contain participial phrases. The imitations are presented as a list of scrambled sentence parts for you to unscramble to duplicate the structure of the model. Unscramble each of the two sentences to produce a sentence similar in structure to the model. Identify the participial phrases in the model and the two imitations. Compare your sentences with the ones in the References on page 174.

> Model: As he ran away into the darkness, they repented of their weakness and ran after him, swearing and throwing sticks and great balls of soft mud at the figure that screamed and ran faster and faster into the darkness.
>
> *Sherwood Anderson*, Winesburg, Ohio

Scrambled Imitations

1a. as her arm whirled fast over the egg-whites

   b. and stared at it

   c. and expressing confusion and frustration over the third direction in the recipe

   d. her face shifted toward the cookbook

   e. grimacing

   f. that listed and explained more and ever more of the procedure

2a. stretching

   b. that beckoned but hid farther and farther from his reach

   c. after Jo-Jo climbed higher onto the counter

   d. but missing jars and boxes in the rear with bright colors

   e. he pulled on the doors

   f. and looked for the candy

Practice 5

Read the model and then the list of sentences underneath it. Combine the list into one sentence having basically the same structure as the model. The order in which the sentences are listed is the order of the sentence parts of the model. In other words, convert the first sentence into the first sentence part of the model, the second sentence into the second part, and so forth. Compare yours with the ones in the References on pages 174–175. Finally, write an imitation of the model with the same structure but your own content.

Example

Model: The horse found the entrance to the trail where it left the flat and started up, **stumbling and slipping on the rocks**.

John Steinbeck, "Flight"

Sentences to Be Combined

1. The cycle hit something.

2. It hit a stretch.

3. The stretch was ice.

4. It happened as it rounded the bend.

5. In addition, it slid sideways.

6. Then it was tottering.

7. In addition, then it was veering.

8. It was veering toward the shoulder.

Combination

The cycle hit a stretch of ice as it rounded the bend and slid sideways, **tottering and veering toward the shoulder**.

Imitation

His arm contacted the concrete of the schoolyard after he missed the jump and landed hard, **snapping and breaking at the impact**.

---

1. Model: The sound of monotonous ax blows rang through the forest, and the insects, **nodding upon their perches**, crooned like old women.

   Stephen Crane, The Red Badge of Courage

   a. A pile of new debris was doing something.

   b. It cluttered up the driveway.

   c. In addition, the tenants were gazing at the disgrace.

   d. They watched with heavy hearts.

2. Model: He stood there, his coat wet, **holding his wet hat**, and said nothing.

   Ernest Hemingway, A Farewell to Arms

   a. The dog did something.

   b. He sat up.

   c. His mouth was clenching the rolled newspaper.

   d. He was wagging his tail.

   e. In addition, he begged a reward.

3. Model: The little shack, the rattling, rotting barn were gray-bitten with sea salt, **beaten by the damp wind until they had taken on the color of the granite hills**.

   John Steinbeck, "Flight"

   a. Something had been done to the upholstered pieces.

   b. Something had been done to the expensive, polished tables.

   c. They had been moved into the huge dining room.

   d. They were covered with endless painter's cloths.

   e. This was done so that they would be protected.

   f. The protection was from the splatterings of paint.

4. Model: The strength that had been as a miracle in her body left, and she half-reeled across the floor, **clutching at the back of the chair in which she had spent so many long**

days staring out over the tin roofs into the main street of Winesburg.

Sherwood Anderson, Winesburg, Ohio

a. The meeting had been like something.

b. It had been like a marathon among meetings.

c. The meeting continued.

d. In addition, the leader deliberated about his strategy.

e. He was stalling after the last remarks from the representative.

f. The representative was the one with whom he had planned something.

g. What they had planned were so many emergency ploys focusing upon every conceivable tactic.

h. The tactic was for the suppression of the opposition.

Practice 6

Write an imitation of each of the models.

Sentence Openers

1. **Taking off his cap**, he placed it over the muzzle of his rifle.

    Liam O'Flaherty, "The Sniper"

2. **Walking forward, watching the bull's feet**, he saw successively his eyes, his wet muzzle, and the wide, forward-pointing spread of his horns.

    Ernest Hemingway, "The Undefeated"

3. **Sitting beside his flowering window while the panes rattled and the wind blew in under the door**, Rosicky gave himself to reflection as he had not done since those Sundays in the loft of the furniture factory in New York, long ago.

    Willa Cather, "Neighbor Rosicky"

Subject-Verb Splits

4. The turkeys, **roosting in the tree out of coyotes' reach**, clucked drowsily.

   John Steinbeck, The Red Pony

5. Her brown face, **upraised**, was stained with tears.

   Stephen Crane, The Red Badge of Courage

6. On September 23 the commissioners, **riding in Army ambulances from Fort Robinson** and **escorted by a somewhat enlarged cavalry troop**, again arrived at the council shelter.

   Dee Brown, Bury My Heart at Wounded Knee

Sentence Closers

7. This land was waterless, **furred with the cacti which could store water and with the great-rooted brush which could reach deep into the earth for a little moisture and get along on very little**.

   John Steinbeck, The Pearl

8. There was good air and light, and I worked quite hard, **skipping rope, shadow-boxing, doing abdominal exercises lying on the floor in a patch of sunlight that came through the open window**, and **occasionally scaring the professor when we boxed**.

   Ernest Hemingway, A Farewell to Arms

9. Nothing else in the world would do but the pure waters which had been summoned from the lakes far away and the sweet fields of grassy dew on early morning, **lifted to the open sky, carried in laundered dusters, brushed with wind, electrified with high voltage**, and **condensed upon cool air**.

   Ray Bradbury, Vintage Bradbury

Multiple Positions

10. She, **thrilled and in part seduced by his words**, instead of resisting as definitely as she would have in any other case, now gazed at him, **fascinated by his enthusiasm**.

    Theodore Dreiser, An American Tragedy

11. Al, **bending over the wheel**, kept shifting eyes from the road to the instrument panel, **watching the ammeter needle**, which jerked suspiciously, **watching the oil gauge and the heat indicator**.

John Steinbeck, The Grapes of Wrath

12. **Soiled by the filth of a strange city, spat upon by unknown mouths, driven from the streets into the roadway, carrying the heaviest loads upon his back, scurrying between carriages, carts, and horses, staring death in the eyes every moment**, he still kept silent.

Isaac Peretz, "Bontsha the Silent"

Practice 7

In the first sentence in each group, a slash mark (/) indicates that the original sentence has a participial phrase at that place. Combine the sentences underneath into a participial phrase that will fit smoothly into that place. Compare your results with the originals in the References on page 175. Write an imitation of the resulting sentences, using your own content but the structure of the model.

Example

a. The little shack, the rattling, rotting barn were gray-bitten with sea salt, / .

b. The shack and the barn were beaten.

c. They were beaten by the damp wind.

d. This happened until they had taken on the color.

e. The color was of the granite hills.

Combination with Participial Phrase

The little shack, the rattling, rotting barn were gray-bitten with sea salt, **beaten by the damp wind until they had taken on the color of the granite hills**.

John Steinbeck, "Flight"

Imitation

The team manager, the surprised, elated team were encouraged, **roused by the roaring fans after the opposing team had fumbled on the fifty-yard line during the last play**.

1a. / , I was wet, cold, and very hungry.

b. I was lying on the floor.

c. The floor was of the flat-car.

d. I was lying with the guns beside me.

e. The guns were under the canvas.

From Ernest Hemingway,
A Farewell to Arms

2a. There was a tattered man, / , who trudged quietly at the youth's side.

b. He was fouled with dust.

c. He was fouled with blood.

d. He was fouled with powder stain.

e. He was fouled from hair to shoes.

From Stephen Crane,
The Red Badge of Courage

3a. I brought the boat up to the stone pier, and the barman pulled in the line, / and / . (two participial phrases)

b. The barman was coiling it.

c. The coiling was on the bottom of the boat.

d. And the barman was hooking the spinner on the edge.

e. The edge was of the gunwale.

From Ernest Hemingway,
A Farewell to Arms

4a. The trail moved up the dry shale hillside, / , / , / . (three participial phrases)

b. The trail was avoiding rocks.

c.   It was dropping under clefts.

d.   It was climbing in and out of something.

e.   The something was old water scars.

From *John Steinbeck, "Flight"*

Practice 8

Combine each list of sentences into one sentence containing a participial phrase. Underline each phrase. You may eliminate words and change their form as long as the intended meaning remains. Punctuate correctly. When you finish, compare your sentences with the originals in the References on pages 175–176.

1a. He was bleeding profusely.

b.   In addition, he was cut off from his supply of eagles' blood.

c.   He had never been closer to death.

From *J. D. Salinger*, Nine Stories

2a. It happened in an upstairs bedroom.

b.   It happened shortly before dawn.

c.   A young American mother sat.

d.   She sat on the edge of a steel-framed bed.

e.   She was rocking her nursing daughter.

From *Steve Estes*, Called to Die

3a. By and by, one group after another came struggling back.

b.   They came straggling back to the mouth of the cave.

c.   They were panting.

d.   They were hilarious.

e.   They were smeared from head to foot with tallow drippings.

f.   They were daubed with clay.

g.   In addition, they were entirely delighted with the success of the day.

From *Mark Twain*,
The Adventures of Tom Sawyer

4a.   Adolph Knipe took a sip of stout.

  b.   He was tasting the malty-bitter flavor.

  c.   He was feeling the trickle of cold liquid.

  d.   He felt the trickle as it traveled down his throat and settled in the top of his stomach.

  e.   At the top of his stomach it was cool at first.

  f.   It was then spreading and becoming warm.

  g.   It was making a little area of warmness inside him.

From *Roald Dahl,*
"The Great Automatic Grammatisator"

Practice 9

Expand the sentences by adding approximately the same number of words the authors used for their participial phrases. The number is next to the slash mark. To help you start, the beginning words of the participial phrases are provided in **boldface**. Compare your participial phrases with the originals in the References on page 176.

1. With the core of the reel showing, his heart feeling stopped with excitement, /11 **leaning** . . ., Nick thumbed the reel hard with his left hand.

Ernest Hemingway, "Big Two-Hearted River"

2. Mrs. Carpenter was putting sun-tan oil on Sybil's shoulders, /11 **spreading**. . . .

J. D. Salinger, Nine Stories

3. Soon the men began to gather, /4 **surveying** . . . , /8 **speaking**. . . .

Shirley Jackson, "The Lottery"

4. The *Carpathia* ship's passengers pitched in gallantly to help the survivors of the *Titanic*, /3 **providing** . . . ,
/2 **lending** . . . , /13 **sewing** . . . .

Walter Lord, A Night to Remember

Practice 10

Add a participial phrase to each of the reduced sentences below, blending your content with the rest of the sentence. Each of the sentences in its original, complete version had a participial phrase in the place indicated by the slash mark. When you finish, compare your sentences with the originals in the References on page 176.

1. The children crawled over the shelves and into the potato and onion bins, / .

   Maya Angelou, I Know Why the Caged Bird Sings

2. And he, / , at once looked over his shoulder at her and, / , signaled that he would meet her.

   Theodore Dreiser, An American Tragedy

3. In the late afternoon, the truck came back, / and / , there was a layer of dust in the bed, and the hood was covered with dust, and the headlights were obscured with a red flour.

   John Steinbeck, The Grapes of Wrath

4. He stood there, / and / , / .

   Roald Dahl, "Beware of the Dog"

*F*ocus 9

Reviewing the Structures

Practice 1

Identify appositive, absolute, or participial phrases. Check your answers in the References on page 177.

1. Now, facing the bull, he was conscious of many things at the same time.

   Ernest Hemingway, "The Undefeated"

2. The writer, an old man with a white mustache, had some difficulty in getting into bed.

   Sherwood Anderson, Winesburg, Ohio

3. Crouched on the edge of the plateau, the schoolmaster looked at the deserted expanse.

   Albert Camus, Exile and the Kingdom

4. His head aching, his throat sore, he forgot to light the cigarette.

   Sinclair Lewis, Cass Timberlane

5. He stood quivering, stiff ears forward, eyes rolling so that the whites showed . . . .

   John Steinbeck, The Red Pony

6. About the bones ants were ebbing away, their pincers full of meat.

   Doris Lessing, African Stories

7. I went over and took a teakwood chair with cushions of emerald-green silk, sitting stiffly with my briefcase across my knees.

   Ralph Ellison, Invisible Man

8. A little house, perched on high piles, appeared black in the distance.

   Joseph Conrad, "The Lagoon"

9. One of eleven brothers and sisters, Harriet was a moody, willful child.

   Langston Hughes, "Road to Freedom"

10. Buck stood and looked on, the successful champion, the dominant primordial beast who had made his kill and found it good.

    Jack London, The Call of the Wild

11. Her gaze, deceiving, transforming her to her imaginings, changed the contour of her sallow-skinned face, re-fashioning her long pointed nose on which a small chilly tear had gathered.

    Brian Moore, The Lonely Passion of Judith Hearne

12. Once Enoch Bentley, the older one of the boys, struck his father, old Tom Bentley, with the butt of a teamster's whip, and the old man seemed likely to die.

    Sherwood Anderson, Winesburg, Ohio

Practice 2

In the following series of tasks, you'll review absolute, appositive, and participial phrases, noticing their differences, uses, and positions.

Task 1
Select a worker—doctor, plumber, artist, teacher, electrician, etc. Next to it, write an absolute phrase, then an appositive phrase, and finally a participial phrase. Put commas before and after the phrases. For example:

1. The handyman, **his tools randomly scattered over the workbench**, (*absolute*)

2. The handyman, **an elderly, neat gentleman with never a grease stain on his work clothes**, (*appositive*)

3. The handyman, **painting over last year's paint on the old lawn furniture**, (*participial*)

Task 2
Write three sentences, using for part of the content the material
you produced in Task 1. For example:

1a. The handyman, **his tools randomly scattered over the
workbench**, tried to make a little order out of the mess by
putting all like things together.

2a. The handyman, **an elderly, neat gentleman with never
a grease stain on his work clothes**, told the distraught
housewife that in just a few minutes he would have things
under control.

3a. The handyman, **painting over last year's paint on the
old lawn furniture**, noticed a paint bubble, got out a
straight pin, pricked it, scraped the loose paint away, then
sanded it smooth.

Task 3
Rewrite the sentences from Task 2 by placing the phrases in the
sentence opener position. In Task 2, they were in the subject-
verb split position. For example:

1b. **His tools randomly scattered over the workbench**, the
handyman tried to make a little order out of the mess by
putting all like things together.

2b. **An elderly, neat gentleman with never a grease stain
on his work clothes**, the handyman told the distraught
housewife that in just a few minutes he would have things
under control.

3b. **Painting over last year's paint on the old lawn
furniture**, the handyman noticed a paint bubble, got out a
straight pin, pricked it, scraped the loose paint away, then
sanded it smooth.

Task 4
The phrases may also occur in the sentence closer position. To
practice their use in this position, retain the three phrases from
the above tasks, but write new content for the rest of each

sentence. Place the name of the worker from the preceding tasks immediately before the phrases. For example:

1c.   Mr. Farley, overseer for landscaping and exteriors at Smithton Estates, criticized the sloppiness of the painter's shed in the maintenance building, and all the while nearby was the handyman, **his tools randomly scattered over the workbench**.

2c.   After ruling out the cook, the baby-sitter, and the boy who cut their lawn, they decided that, with their unfortunate fallen financial state, they could only keep in their hire the handyman, **an elderly, neat gentleman with never a grease stain on his work clothes**.

3c.   While she was stretching the lace curtains out in the backyard, he was putting old clothes in boxes to give to Goodwill; and paying no attention to either was the handyman, **painting over last year's paint on the old lawn furniture**.

Task 5

Select one of your sentences containing an absolute phrase and add another absolute phrase. Do the same with the appositive and participial phrases. For example:

1d.   The handyman, **his tools randomly scattered over the workbench, his hands moving determinedly**, tried to make a little order out of the mess by putting all like things together.

2d.   After ruling out the cook, the baby-sitter, and the boy who cut their lawn, they decided that, with their unfortunate fallen financial state, they could only keep in their hire the handyman, **an elderly, neat gentleman with never a grease stain on his work clothes, a man in their employ for over two generations**.

3d.   The handyman, **painting over last year's paint on the old lawn furniture, acting upon his reputation as a perfectionist**, noticed a paint bubble, got out a straight pin, pricked it, scraped the loose paint away, then sanded it smooth.

Practice 3

For each worker listed, write a sentence of at least twenty words describing the worker on the job. Include, underline, and punctuate the phrase described in parentheses.

1. Bartender (sentence opener, absolute)

2. Jockey (subject-verb split, absolute)

3. Newspaper boy (sentence closer, absolute)

4. Bank teller (sentence opener, appositive)

5. Baby-sitter (subject-verb split, appositive)

6. Fireman (sentence closer, appositive)

7. Actor (sentence opener, participial)

8. Model (subject-verb split, participial)

9. Taxi driver (sentence closer, participial)

10. Cashier at a supermarket (sentence opener, two absolutes)

11. Secretary (subject-verb split, two absolutes)

12. Teacher (sentence closer, two absolutes)

13. Dancer (sentence opener, two appositives)

14. Writer (subject-verb split, two appositives)

15. Truck driver (sentence closer, two appositives)

16. Detective (sentence opener, two participials)

17. Salesperson (subject-verb split , two participials)

18. Waitress (sentence closer, two participles)

19. Artist (one of each—absolute, appositive, and participial— in any order, in any position)

Practice 4

The list of sentences below illustrates the combination of phrases (absolutes, appositives, participials) within a sentence. Combinations are common in professional writing and worth using wisely in your own.

  Identify the types of phrases in **boldface**. Check your answers in the References on pages 177–178. Next, write six imitations, using any two models you choose from each group of sentence lengths—short, medium, long. For your six sentences, imitate the structure and length of the models but use your own content.

Short Sentences

1. **Gasping, his hands raw**, he reached a flat place at the top.

   Richard Connell, "The Most Dangerous Game"

2. He stood there, **his coat wet, holding his wet hair**, and said nothing.

   Ernest Hemingway, A Farewell to Arms

3. He stood quivering, **stiff ears forward, eyes rolling so that the whites showed, pretending to be frightened**.

   John Steinbeck, The Red Pony

4. He walked in the rain, **an old man with his hat off, a carabinieri on either side**.

   Ernest Hemingway, A Farewell to Arms

Medium Sentences

5. **One of many small groups of children, each child carrying his little bag of crackling**, we trod the long road home in the cold winter afternoon.

   Peter Abrahams, Tell Freedom

6. It ran, **its pelvic bones crushing aside trees and bushes, its taloned feet clawing damp earth, leaving prints six inches deep wherever it settled its weight**.

   Ray Bradbury, A Sound of Thunder

7. I turned to "Annabel Lee," and we walked up and down the garden rows, **the cool dirt between our toes, reciting the beautifully sad lines**.

   Maya Angelou, I Know Why the Caged Bird Sings

8. The masters were in their places for the first Chapel, **seated in stalls in front of and at right angles to us, suggesting by their worn expressions and careless postures that they had never been away at all**.

   John Knowles, A Separate Peace

Long Sentences

9. The midwife, **arriving late**, had found the baby's head pulled out of shape, **its neck stretched, its body warped**; and she had pushed the head back and molded the body with her hands.

   John Steinbeck, The Grapes of Wrath

10. He trembled alone there in the middle of the park for hours, **wondering what would happen if he had an attack of appendicitis, unnerved by the thoughts of a fainting spell, horrified by the realization that he might have to move his bowels**, until at last we came.

    John Knowles, A Separate Peace

11. Out in the distance the fans of windmills twinkled, **turning**, and about the base of each, about the drink tank, was a speckle of dark dots, **a herd of cattle, grazing in moonlight** and **meditating upon good grass, block salt, impermanence, and love**.

    Glendon Swarthout, Bless the Beasts and Children

12. The day my son Laurie started kindergarten he renounced corduroy overalls with bibs and began wearing blue jeans with a belt; I watched him go off the first morning with the older girl next door, **seeing clearly that an era of my life was ended, my sweet-voiced nursery-school tot replaced by a long-trousered, swaggering character who forgot to stop at the corner and wave good-bye to me**.

    Shirley Jackson, "Charles"

3

Varying Professional Positions

"Word carpentry is like any other kind of carpentry: you must build your sentences smoothly."

Anatole France

Throughout *Sentence Composing for College* you have been apprenticing in how to build better sentences, learning the tools that professional writers use to achieve sentence variety.

In this part of the worktext you'll learn how those writers fill three positions in their sentences: the beginning (*sentence opener*), the slot between a subject and verb (*subject-verb split*), and the ending (*sentence closer*). The use of these three positions is common in professional writing, rare in student writing. The goal of the practices that follow is to bridge that gap by focusing on how professional writers achieve variety by using sentence openers, subject-verb splits, and sentence closers.

You'll study sentences that use those positions to create their architecture. You'll learn how their writers create their interior design. Finally, you'll understand that building better sentences is a result of structure and content, of style and substance, of subject and strategy—of architecture and of interior design.

Sentence composing is a craft.

"We are all apprentices in a craft where no one ever becomes a master."

Ernest Hemingway

*F*ocus 10

Sentence Openers

Here's a list of sentences, all written by professional writers, but with some parts deleted.

1. The outlook was anything but bright.
2. No more than six or seven were out on the cold, open platform.
3. He started along the main corridor on his way toward the stairs.
4. Manuel noticed the points of the bull's horns.
5. Elizabeth Willard lighted a lamp and put it on a dressing table that stood by the door.

Now compare the sentences above with the originals below. Notice that it's the **boldface** parts (sentence openers) that account for the professional sentence variety.

1a. **With the newcomers hopeless and forlorn, and the old team worn out by twenty-five hundred miles of continuous trail**, the outlook was anything but bright.
   Jack London, The Call of the Wild

2a. **Of the twenty-some young men who were waiting at the station for their dates to arrive on the 10:52**, no more than six or seven were out on the cold, open platform.
   J. D. Salinger, Franny and Zooey

3a. **With the blood specimen in his left hand, walking in a kind of distraction that he had felt all morning, probably because of the dream and his restless night**, he started along the main corridor on his way toward the stairs.
   John Hersey, Hiroshima

4a. **Standing still now and spreading the red cloth of the muleta with the sword, pricking the point into the**

cloth so that the sword, now held in his left hand, spread the red flannel like the jib of a boat, Manuel noticed the points of the bull's horns.

Ernest Hemingway, "The Undefeated"

5a. **In her room, tucked away in a corner of the old Willard house**, Elizabeth Willard lighted a lamp and put it on a dressing table that stood by the door.

Sherwood Anderson, Winesburg, Ohio

Definition of a Sentence Opener

A sentence opener is any structure that occupies the opening position of a sentence. Here are examples:

1. **Alone**, I would often speak to her. . . .
Henry Miller, Stand Still Like the Hummingbird

2. **Milky and opaque**, it has the pinkish bloom of the sky. . . .
Anne Morrow Lindbergh, Gift from the Sea

3. **At the gate**, I show the pass to a young Japanese private. . . .
Richard E. Kim, Lost Names

4. **On Monday afternoons, when we are allowed to have visitors**, the tent is packed with parents and relatives. . . .
Richard E. Kim, Lost Names

5. **Suffering, sick, and angry, but also grimly satisfied with his new stoicism**, he stood there leaning on his rifle. . . .
Doris Lessing, "A Sunrise on the Veld" from African Stories

Practice 1

Unscramble the sentence parts to produce a sentence with a sentence opener. Some sentences have more than one sentence opener; for those, decide the best order. Punctuate correctly, with a comma after each sentence opener. Compare your results with the professional writers' sentences in the References on page 178.

1a.   that I have ever experienced anywhere

 b.   and the reporters fired questions

 c.   in the biggest press conference

 d.   the camera bulbs flashed
   Malcolm X, (with Alex Haley) The Autobiography of Malcolm X

2a.   of paper

 b.   without a word

 c.   she took a piece

 d.   out of her pants pocket
   Richard E. Kim, Lost Names

3a.   but the most innocent pleasure

 b.   even then

 c.   our shyness prevented us from sharing anything

 d.   when we might have kissed and embraced unrestrainedly
   Henry Miller, Stand Still Like the Hummingbird

4a.   I heard their laughter crackling and popping

 b.   in a cooking stove

 c.   before the girls got to the porch

 d.   like pine logs
   Maya Angelou, I Know Why the Caged Bird Sings

5a.   in a dreamlike state of mind

 b.   through the burial in Pleasant Memory Cemetery and the car trip home,

 c.   who stopped by afterward,

 d.   through the flurry of reclaiming the children, setting up the coffeepot, and greeting the guests

 e.   Ian wandered
   Anne Tyler, Saint Maybe

6a.   and her children

 b.   being a star in her own right

c.   she was well able

d.   earning twenty-five pounds a week

e.   to support herself

Charlie Chaplin, My Autobiography

7a.   facing the bull

b.   at the same time

c.   he was conscious

d.   now

e.   of many things

Ernest Hemingway, "The Undefeated"

8a.   but like something he had never even imagined

b.   was a figure from a dream

c.   there

d.   a strange beast that was horned and drunken-legged

e.   between two trees

f.   against a background of gaunt black rocks

Doris Lessing, "A Sunrise on the Veld"

Practice 2

Identify any structures that could become sentence openers and rearrange each sentence so that it has a sentence opener. Compare yours with the originals in the References on page 179.

Scrambled Sentences

1. My turn came at last, after what seemed hours.

Peter Abrahams, Tell Freedom

2. Other children trotted in twos and threes, behind and in front of us.

Peter Abrahams, Tell Freedom

3. Everything was perfect, even the punctuation, on the very next try a few days later.

Roald Dahl, "The Great Automatic Grammatisator"

4. He had persuaded something like seventy percent of the writers on his list to sign the contract in the end, after several months of work.

   Roald Dahl, "The Great Automatic Grammatisator"

5. A fat little old man walked nervously up and down upon the half decayed veranda of a small frame house that stood near the edge of a ravine near the town of Winesburg, Ohio.

   Sherwood Anderson, Winesburg, Ohio

6. He stood there leaning on his rifle, and watched the seething black mound grow smaller, suffering, sick, and angry, but also grimly satisfied with his new stoicism.

   Doris Lessing, "A Sunrise on the Veld"
   from African Stories

Practice 3

Unscramble each list to produce a sentence similar in structure to the model. The model sentence contains *two* sentence openers, one at the beginning of each of the two main clauses in the sentence. Compare yours with the ones in the References on page 179.

> Model: **In the city, when the word came to him**, he walked about at night through the streets thinking of the matter, and **when he had come home and had got the work on the farm well under way**, he went again at night to walk through the forests and over the low hills and to think of God.
>
> *Sherwood Anderson*, Winesburg, Ohio

Scrambled Imitations

1a. they emptied it out in minutes piling up the garbage

 b. and to shift with thuds

 c. at the dumpster

 d. and as they pulled away and started the turn near Canal Street much too fast

 e. when the truck arrived with junk

f.   the remaining debris began to clank in the back and near the cabin

2a. from the start

 b. he dragged himself at eight o'clock to open up the store and the prepayment office

 c. because the store had opened with haste

 d. and because he had been up late last night and had the alarm in the morning set too late

 e. Jackson pondered constantly in dread during the day wondering about his boss

 f. and to worry over his possible punishment

Practice 4

Combine the list into one sentence having basically the same sentence structure as the model. Compare yours with the ones in the References on pages 179–180. Finally, write an imitation of the model with the same structure as the model but your own content.

Example

> Model: **About a year later, when I had returned from the West, sadder and wiser, to return to the arms of "the widow" from whom I had run away**, we met again by chance.
>   *Henry Miller*, Stand Still Like the Hummingbird

Sentences to Be Combined

a. It happened almost an hour ago.

b. It happened as I was mowing the lawn.

c. I was tired and dirty.

d. The mowing of the lawn was to spruce up the appearance of the property.

e. The property was one in which I had heavily invested.

f. The real estate agent arrived with the house-hunters.

Combination

Almost an hour ago, as I was mowing the lawn, tired and dirty, to spruce up the appearance of the property in which I had heavily invested, the real estate agent arrived with the house-hunters.

Imitation

Around the same time, when he had wrapped the manuscript, weary but satisfied, to mail it to the editor with whom he had discussed revisions, he talked twice with the advertising director.

1. Model: **While touring with this company**, she met and ran off with the middle-aged lord to Africa.

   Charlie Chaplin, My Autobiography

   a. This incident occurred after a meeting.

   b. The meeting was with the President.

   c. He signed the letter after meeting with the President.

   d. He delivered the letter.

   e. The person to whom he delivered it was the secretary.

2. Model: **When I came back in the store**, I took Momma's hand, and we both walked outside to look at the pattern.

   Maya Angelou, I Know Why the Caged Bird Sings

   a. It happened after she tried something.

   b. What she tried was the choreography.

   c. She met the director.

   d. In addition, they planned to confer with someone.

   e. The person they planned to confer with was the producer.

3. Model: **In all the mornings and evenings of the winter months**, young and old, big and small, were helpless victims of the bitter cold.

   Peter Abrahams, Tell Freedom

a. It happened through all the ups of the trial.

b. Also, it happened through all the downs of the trial.

c. The lawyers and the judge had done something.

d. Also, the defendant and the jury had done something.

e. All of them had been listeners.

f. Their listening was intense.

g. What they listened to was the expert testimony.

4. Model: **Too tired to help the bush boy with fire making, and too worn-out to eat,** he crawled wearily across his sister, put his head on her lap, and fell instantly asleep.

James V. Marshall, Walkabout

a. Miss Simpson was too pleasant to fight.

b. The fight would have been with the customer.

c. The fight would have been about the return.

d. In addition, Miss Simpson was too agreeable to resist.

e. Miss Simpson agreed with a smile.

f. She refunded the money without protest.

g. Also, she remained remarkably calm.

Practice 5

Following the structure of the model sentence, but using your own content, write a sentence imitation of each of the models below. Imitate the structure of the entire sentence, not just the sentence opener.

1. **In all the years which have since elapsed**, she remains the woman I loved and lost, the unattainable one.

Henry Miller, Stand Still Like the Hummingbird

2. **When we had made our way downstairs**, we saw the woman with the lovely complexion, Miss Pilzer, screaming and begging to be allowed to go with her mother.

Gerda Weissmann Klein, All But My Life

3. **Often, walking home at night, after having made a tour of her house**, I would yell her name aloud, imploringly, as if to beg her to grant me the favour of an audience from on high.

   Henry Miller, Stand Still Like the Hummingbird

4. **Never having enjoyed, to any considerable extent, her soothing presence, her tender and watchful care**, I received the tidings of her death with much the same emotions I should have probably felt at the death of a stranger.

   Frederick Douglass, "A Slave's Beginning"

5. **In my robe and barefoot in the backyard, under cover of going to see about my new beans**, I gave myself up to the gentle warmth and thanked God that no matter what evil I had done in my life He had allowed me to live to see this day.

   Maya Angelou, I Know Why the Caged Bird Sings

6. **Like a boil that can never be cured so long as it is covered up but must be opened with all its ugliness to the natural medicines of air and light**, injustice must be exposed, with all the tension its exposure creates, to the light of human conscience and the air of natural opinion before it can be cured.

   Martin Luther King, Jr., "Letter from Birmingham Jail"

Practice 6

Change the sentence(s) underneath the first sentence into sentence openers to insert at the slash mark. Compare your sentences with the originals in the References on page 180. After you've combined the sentences into one, write an imitation of the resulting sentence, with your own content but the structure of the model.

Example

a. / , Doctor Parcival began to walk up and down in the office of the *Winesburg Eagle*, where George Willard sat listening.

b. Doctor Parcival was jumping to his feet and breaking off the tale.

Combination with Sentence Openers

Jumping to his feet and breaking off the tale, Doctor Parcival began to walk up and down in the office of the *Winesburg Eagle*, where George Willard sat listening.

Sherwood Anderson, Winesburg, Ohio

Imitation

Gaining on the front-runner and pulling out all the stops, number thirteen started to swing wide from the rest of the horses, where the track was sloppier.

1a. / , the manuscript had been read and accepted by an enthusiastic publisher.

b. This happened within a week.

From *Roald Dahl,*
"The Great Automatic Grammatisator"

2a. /, the German submarines arrived in the middle of the night.

b. The submarines were like silent, hungry sharks that swim in the darkness of the sea.

From *Theodore Taylor*, The Cay

3a. /, Rosicky gave himself to reflection as he had not done since those Sundays in the loft of the furniture factory in New York, long ago.

b. Rosicky was sitting beside his flowering window while the panes rattled and the wind blew in under the door.

From *Willa Cather, "Neighbor Rosicky"*

4a. /, the schoolmaster looked at the deserted expanse.

b. The schoolmaster was crouched on the edge of the plateau.

From *Albert Camus, "The Guest"*

5a. /, /, he felt as if he could squeal or laugh out loud.

b. His feet were sinking in the soft nap of the carpet.

c. His hand was in one pocket clutching the money.

From *Theodore Dreiser*, An American Tragedy

6a. /, /, /, /, /, /, he still kept silent.

  b.   He was soiled by the filth of a strange city.

  c.   He was spat upon by unknown mouths.

  d.   He was driven from the streets into the roadway.

  e.   He was carrying the heaviest loads upon his back.

  f.   He was scurrying between carriages, carts, and horses.

  g.   He was staring death in the eyes every moment.

From Isaac Peretz, "Bontsha the Silent"

Practice 7

Combine each list of sentences into one sentence containing a sentence opener(s). You may eliminate words, or change their form, so long as the intended meaning remains. Compare your work with the originals in the References on pages 180–181.

1a.   Something happens when a man remains single.

  b.   He converts himself into a temptation.

  c.   The temptation is permanent.

  d.   The temptation is public.

From Oscar Wilde

2a.   Pain was shooting.

  b.   It was shooting up my entire arm.

  c.   I lay panting.

  d.   I panted on the edge of the pool.

  e.   In addition, I gingerly began to feel my wrist.

From Theodore Taylor, The Cay

3a.   Gumbril was pretending to take an interest.

  b.   The interest was in the New Season's Models.

  c.   Gumbril was squinting sideways over the burning tip of his cigar.

   d.   While doing these things, he made an inventory.

   e.   The inventory was of her features.
From Aldous Huxley, Antic Hay

4a.   It happened in the frosty December dusk.

   b.   Their cabins looked neat and snug with pale blue smoke rising.

   c.   It was rising from the chimneys.

   d.   Their cabins looked neat and snug with doorways glowing.

   e.   The doorways were glowing amber from the fires inside.
From Harper Lee, To Kill a Mockingbird

5a.   It happened in the darkness.

   b.   The darkness was in the hallway.

   c.   The hallway was by the door.

   d.   The sick woman arose.

   e.   In addition, the sick woman started again toward her own room.
From Sherwood Anderson, Winesburg, Ohio

6a.   It happened in her girlhood.

   b.   It happened also before her marriage.

   c.   Her marriage was with Tom Willard.

   d.   What happened was that Elizabeth had borne a somewhat shaky reputation.

   e.   The reputation was in Winesburg.
From Sherwood Anderson, Winesburg, Ohio

7a.   It happened near the edge of town.

   b.   What happened was that the group had to walk around an automobile.

   c.   The automobile was burned and squatting on the narrow road.

   d.   In addition, the bearers on one side fell.

e.   They were unable to see their way in the darkness.

f.   They fell into a deep ditch.

From *John Hersey*, Hiroshima

8a.   It happened by nightfall of an average courting day.

b.   A certain kind of fiddler crab then was in pretty sad shape.

c.   The certain kind is one who has been standing on tiptoe.

d.   The standing took place for eight or ten hours.

e.   While standing, it was waving a heavy claw.

f.   The waving was in the air.

From *James Thurber,*
"Courtship Through the Ages"

Practice 8

Add sentence openers to each of the reduced sentences below. Each of the sentences, in their complete versions, has sentence openers in the places indicated by slash marks. When you finish, compare your sentences with the originals in the References on pages 181–182.

Example

Reduced Sentence:

 /, /, Tarzan took to the trees in search of game.

Student-Expanded Sentence:

With Jane and Boy to provide for now, both hungry after their ordeal with the wild animals, Tarzan took to the trees in search of game.

Original Sentence

Later in the day, his rope repaired, Tarzan took to the trees in search of game.

Edgar Rice Burroughs, "Tarzan's First Love"

---

1.   /, we rode to the hospital in a carriage with a horse.

Frank McCourt, Angela's Ashes

2. /, she had many beaux, but these small-town boys didn't interest her.

   Willa Cather, "Coming, Aphrodite!"

3. /, the tall dark girl had been in those days much confused.

   Sherwood Anderson, Winesburg, Ohio

4. /, they threaded the shimmering channel in the rowboat and, tying it to a jutting rock, began climbing the cliff together.

   F. Scott Fitzgerald, Flappers and Philosophers

5. /, the truck came back, bumping and rattling through the dust, and there was a layer of dust in the bed, and the hood was covered with dust, and the headlights were obscured with a red flour.

   John Steinbeck, The Grapes of Wrath

6. /, /, an invitation out meant an evening in other people's lives, and therefore freedom from his own, and it meant the possibility of laughter that would surprise him—how good it was to be alive and healthy, to have a body that had not given up in spite of everything.

   Joyce Carol Oates, "The Wheel of Love"

7. /, /, she would still keep her eyes closed for a long time, then open them and relish with astonishment the blue of the brand-new curtains, replacing the apricot-pink which had filtered the morning light into the room where she had slept as a girl.

   Colette, "The Hand"

8. /, /, /, Dr. Sasaki lost all sense of profession and stopped working as a skillful surgeon and a sympathetic man; he became an automaton, mechanically wiping, daubing, winding, wiping, daubing, winding.

   John Hersey, Hiroshima

Practice 9

From a recent piece of writing of your own, select five sentences that do not begin with sentence openers. Add them.

*F*ocus 11

Subject-Verb Splits

Here's a list of sentences, all written by well-known writers, but with some parts deleted.

1. Her hair made an ash-blond crown.

2. The all-powerful auto industry was suddenly forced to *listen* for a change.

3. Their restless activity had given him his name.

4. Henry Strader made the same joke every morning.

5. The coming of industrialism has worked a tremendous change in the lives and in the habits of thought of our people of Mid-America.

Now compare the sentences above with the originals below. Notice that it's the **boldface** parts (subject-verb splits) that account for the professional sentence variety.

1a. Her hair, **braided and wrapped around her head**, made an ash-blond crown.
   John Steinbeck, The Grapes of Wrath

2a. The all-powerful auto industry, **accustomed to telling the customer what sort of car he wanted**, was suddenly forced to *listen* for a change.
   Jessica Mitford, The American Way of Death

3a. Their restless activity, **like unto the beating of the wings of an imprisoned bird**, had given him his name.
   Sherwood Anderson, Winesburg, Ohio

4a. Henry Strader, **an old man who had been on the farm since Jesse came into possession and who before David's time had never been known to make a joke**, made the same joke every morning.
   Sherwood Anderson, Winesburg, Ohio

5a. The coming of industrialism, **attended by all the roar and rattle of affairs, the shrill cries of millions of new voices that have come among us from overseas, the going and coming of trains, the growth of cities, the building of the inter-urban car lines that weave in and out of towns and past farm-houses, and now in these days the coming of automobiles**, has worked a tremendous change in the lives and in the habits of thought of our people of Mid-America.

Sherwood Anderson, Winesburg, Ohio

Definition of a Subject-Verb Split

A subject-verb split is any structure that occupies the position between the subject and the verb of a sentence. Here are examples:

1. A sigh, **short and faint**, marked an almost imperceptible pause, and then his words flowed on, without a stir, without a gesture.

Joseph Conrad, "The Lagoon"

2. Poppa, **a good quiet man**, spent the last hours before our parting moving aimlessly about the yard, keeping to himself and avoiding me.

Gordon Parks, "My Mother's Dream for Me"

3. The Russians, **coming from streets around the cemetery**, were hurrying, singly or in groups, in the spring snow in the direction of the caves in the ravine, some running in the middle of the slushy cobblestone streets.

Bernard Malamud, The Fixer

4. Such goings-on, **though of great antiquity**, still have the power to shock the more piously orthodox.

Thomas Cahill, How the Irish Saved Civilization

5. This leader, **whose word was law among boys who defied authority for the sake of defiance**, was no more than twelve or thirteen years old and looked even younger.

Henry G. Felsen, "Horatio"

Practice 1

Unscramble the sentence parts to produce a sentence with a subject-verb split. Punctuate correctly, with one comma before the subject-verb split and one after. Compare your results with the professional writers' sentences in the References on page 182.

1a.   in getting into bed

 b.   the writer

 c.   had some difficulty

 d.   an old man with a white mustache
>   *Sherwood Anderson*, Winesburg, Ohio

2a.   suddenly arose and advanced toward him

 b.   absorbed in his own idea

 c.   his terror grew until his whole body shook

 d.   when Jesse Bentley
>   *Sherwood Anderson*, Winesburg, Ohio

3a.   the twins

 b.   in a detached way

 c.   smeary in the face, eating steadily from untidy paper sacks of sweets

 d.   followed them
>   *Katherine Anne Porter*, Ship of Fools

4a.   the sinuous, limbless body

 b.   his hands

 c.   ran up and down the soft-skinned baby body

 d.   beyond control
>   *Judith Merrill, "That Only a Mother"*

5a.   one of them

 b.   talked continually

c.   a slender young man with white hands, the son of a jeweler in Winesburg

d.   of virginity
Sherwood Anderson, Winesburg, Ohio

6a.   felt more pleasure than pain

b.   fresh from the pounding of Johnnie's fists

c.   his face

d.   and the driving snow

e.   in the wind
Stephen Crane, "The Blue Hotel"

7a.   with the knotted, cracked joints and the square, horn-thick nails

b.   the big hands

c.   of a shed after work

d.   hang loose off the wrist bone

e.   hung on the wall

f.   like clumsy, homemade tools
Robert Penn Warren,
"The Patented Gate and the Mean Hamburger"

8a.   who had brought flowers and baskets of fruit

b.   took leisurely leave

c.   their dark hair sleeked down over their ears, their thin-soled black slippers too short in the toes and badly run over at high heels

d.   of a half dozen local young men

e.   the four pretty, slatternly Spanish girls

f.   with kisses all around
Katherine Anne Porter, Ship of Fools

Practice 2

Unscramble each list to produce a sentence similar in structure to the model. The model contains *two* subject-verb splits, one in each of the two main clauses. Compare yours with the ones in the References on page 183.

> Model: In the presence of George Willard, Wing Biddlebaum, **who for twenty years had been the town mystery**, lost something of his timidity, and his shadowy personality, **submerged in a sea of doubts**, came forth to look at the world.
>   *Sherwood Anderson*, Winesburg, Ohio

Scrambled Imitations

1a. warned the traffic to make way

  b. in the flurry of traffic

  c. who only an hour ago had been asleep

  d. wailing like a giant in agony

  e. the ambulance driver

  f. and his siren

  g. gripped the steering wheel

2a. derived from this year's self-control with alcohol

  b. near the field of wheat

  c. who a year ago had been an irresponsible drunk

  d. tough-skinned Jasper

  e. allowed him to concentrate on farming

  f. and his serenity

  g. walked peacefully among his crops

Practice 3

Combine the list into one sentence having basically the same sentence structure as the model. Compare yours with the ones in the References on page 183. Finally, write an imitation of the model with the same structure as the model but your own content.

Example

Model: At daybreak Rainsford, **lying near the swamp**, was awakened by a sound that made him know that he had new things to learn about fear.

Richard Connell, "The Most Dangerous Game"

Sentences to Be Combined

a. It occurred before the game.

b. Winston was the one to whom it happened.

c. He was suffering from nervousness.

d. Winston was telephoned.

e. A fellow player called him.

f. It was the player who told him something.

g. What he told Winston was that Winston had several plays to revise.

h. The revision had to take place before the game.

Combination

Before the game Winston, **suffering from nervousness**, was telephoned by a fellow player who told him that Winston had several plays to revise before the game.

Imitation

Near the junkyard Mr. Pauley, **jogging through the intersection**, was surprised by a truck that made him realize that he should change his route to arrive after dawn.

---

1. Model: Van'ka Zhukov, **a boy of nine who had been apprenticed to the shoemaker Alyakhin three months ago**, was staying up that Christmas eve.

Anton Chekhov, "Van'ka"

a. Nielsen Rating Service was in operation.

b. This service was a determiner of TV ratings.

c. They were the ratings that had been accepted by the TV networks that season.

d. The operation the service was engaged in was surveying this morning.

2. Model: Dvoira, **the dark-uddered cow**, was out in the field behind the hut, browsing under a leafless poplar tree, and Yakov went out to her.

> *Bernard Malamud*, The Fixer

a. The cook was a fine-bellied gourmet.

b. He was back in the kitchen at the closet freezer.

c. He was ruminating about the latest beef selections.

d. In addition, the butcher reassured him.

3. Model: When his father, **who was old and twisted with toil**, made over to him the ownership of the farm and seemed content to creep away to a corner and wait for death, he shrugged his shoulders and dismissed the old man from his mind.

> *Sherwood Anderson*, Winesburg, Ohio

a. It happened because the thunder-storm did something.

b. It was one which was sudden and fierce in downpour.

c. It brought to fields the rain for the crops.

d. In addition, it was steady enough to remain in the parched land and penetrate to the roots.

e. The result was that the plants raised their branches.

f. Another result was that they arched their stems toward the sun.

4. Model: Warren McIntyre, **who casually attended Yale, being one of the unfortunate stags**, felt in his dinner-coat pocket for a cigarette and strolled out onto the wide, semi-

dark veranda, where couples were scattered at tables, filling the lantern-hung night with vague words and hazy laughter.

F. Scott Fitzgerald, "Bernice Bobs Her Hair"

a. The sentence concerns Janice Larson.

b. She was one who successfully finished auto-mechanics.

c. She had been one of few girls in the course.

d. She tried with great persistence for a related job.

e. In addition, she applied to several employment agencies.

f. At those agencies, counselors were surprised at her sex.

g. They described her prospects.

h. The description of her prospects was done with guarded optimism and sincere hope.

Practice 4

Following the structure of the model sentence, but using your own content, write a sentence imitation of each of the models below. Imitate the structure of the entire sentence, not just the subject-verb split.

1. Paul Maugé, **the chef's assistant**, jumped 10 feet from the *Titanic* into a dangling boat.

   Walter Lord, A Night to Remember

2. In the late afternoon Will Henderson, **owner and editor of the Eagle**, went over to Tom Willy's saloon.

   Sherwood Anderson, Winesburg, Ohio

3. Yakov, **in loose clothes and peaked cap**, was an elongated nervous man with large ears, stained hard hands, a broad back and tormented face, lightened a bit by gray eyes and brownish hair.

   Bernard Malamud, The Fixer

4. Over yonder, the Schenley, **in its vacant stretch**, loomed big and square through the fine rain, the windows of its

twelve stories glowing like those of a lighted cardboard house under a Christmas tree.

Willa Cather, "Paul's Case"

5. The Russians, **coming from streets around the cemetery**, were hurrying, singly or in groups, in the spring snow in the direction of the caves in the ravine, some running in the middle of the slushy cobblestone streets.

Bernard Malamud, The Fixer

6. And so it was that Roberta, **after encouraging Clyde and sensing the superior world in which she imagined he moved, and being so taken with the charm of his personality**, was seized with the very virus of ambition and unrest that afflicted him.

Theodore Dreiser, An American Tragedy

Practice 5

Change the second sentence into a subject-verb split to insert at the slash mark. Compare your sentences with the originals in the References on pages 183–184. After you have combined the two sentences into one, write an imitation of the resulting sentence with your own content but the structure of the model.

Example

a. The Cavaliere, /, had lighted another candle.

b. The Cavaliere felt refreshed.

Combination with Subject-Verb Split

The Cavaliere, **refreshed**, had lighted another candle.

Thomas Mann, "Mario and the Magician"

Imitation

The jockey, **exhausted**, had won another race.

1a.   The other sniper, /, thought that he had killed his man.

 b.   He thought so because he was seeing the cap and rifle fall.

From Liam O'Flaherty, "The Sniper"

2a.　Manuel, /, felt there was someone in the room.

　b.　Manuel was standing in the hallway.
　　　　　　　From *Ernest Hemingway, "The Undefeated"*

3a.　The bull, /, pivoted and charged the cape, his head down, his tail rising.

　b.　The bull was in full gallop.
　　　　　　　From *Ernest Hemingway, "The Undefeated"*

4a.　The members of the cuadrilla, /, came walking back and stood in a group talking, under the electric light in the patio.

　b.　The members were those who had been watching the burlesque from the runway between the barrera and the seats.
　　　　　　　From *Ernest Hemingway, "The Undefeated"*

5a.　He found that the older ones, /, were the easiest to handle.

　b.　Those who were easiest to handle were the ones who were running out of ideas and had taken to drink.
　　　　　　　From *Roald Dahl, "The Great Automatic*
　　　　　　　Grammatisator"

6a.　A succession of loud and shrill screams, /, seemed to thrust me violently back.

　b.　These screams burst suddenly from the throat of the chained form.
　　　　　　　From *Edgar Allan Poe, "The Cask of Amontillado"*

Practice 6

Add appropriate short subject-verb splits to each of the reduced sentences below. Each of the sentences in this group, in its original complete version, has short subject-verb splits—five words or fewer. When you finish, compare your sentences with the originals in the References on page 184. The place for your insert is indicated with a slash mark.

Example

Reduced Sentence

A little house, /, appeared black in the distance.

Student-Expanded Sentence

A little house, **abandoned and overrun with weeds**, appeared black in the distance.

Original Sentence

A little house, **perched on high piles**, appeared black in the distance.

Joseph Conrad, "The Lagoon"

1. When the match went out, the old man, /, peeped into the little window.

   Anton Chekhov, "The Bet"

2. The country house, /, was most enjoyable.

   James Thurber, "Mr. Monroe Holds the Fort"

3. At once Buntaro slid an arrow from the quiver and, /, set up the bow, raised it, drew back the bowstring to eye level and released the shaft with savage, almost poetic liquidity.

   James Clavell, Shogun

4. These three trains, /, confirmed my fears that traffic was not maintained by night on this part of the line.

   Winston Churchill, "I Escape from the Boers"

5. The first opportune minute came that very afternoon, and Cress, /, went in tears to her room.

   Jessamyn West, "Cress Delahanty"

6. And my departure, which, /, stank of betrayal, was my only means of proving, or redeeming, that love, my only hope.

   James Baldwin, "Every Good-bye Ain't Gone"

7. Only a frying pan, /, remained.

   Naomi Hintze, "The Lost Gold of Superstitions"

8. (Contains two.) His little dark eyes, /, and his mouth, /, made him look attentive and studious.

   Albert Camus, Exile and the Kingdom

Practice 7

Add subject-verb splits to each sentence below. Each of the sentences in this group, in its original complete version, has medium subject-verb splits—six to fifteen words. Compare your sentences with the originals in the References on pages 184–185.

Example

Reduced Sentence

> There was also a rhino, who, /, came there each night.

Student-Expanded Sentence

> There was also a rhino, who, **thirsty from having had no water since the rainy season a month ago**, came there each night.

Original Sentence

> There was also a rhino, who, **from the tracks and the kicked-up mound of strawy dung**, came there each night.
> *Ernest Hemingway*, Green Hills of Africa

---

1. During the first year of imprisonment, the lawyer, /, suffered terribly from loneliness and boredom.
   Anton Chekhov, "The Bet"

2. While we were waiting for the coffee, the headwaiter, /, came up to us bearing a large basket full of huge peaches.
   W. Somerset Maugham, "The Luncheon"

3. Doubletree Mutt came sideways and embarrassed up through the vegetable patch, and Jody, /, put his arm about the dog's neck and kissed him on his wide black nose.
   John Steinbeck, The Red Pony

4. Her gaze, /, changed the contour of her sallow-skinned face, skillfully refashioning her long-pointed nose on which a small chilly tear had gathered.
   Brian Moore, The Lonely Passion of Judith Hearne

5. She, /, now gazed at him, fascinated by his enthusiasm.
   Theodore Dreiser, An American Tragedy

6. The mouth-organist, /, got up and began dancing up and down the aisle, playing the instrument with one hand and flouncing up her skirts with the other as she jiggled in time to an old music-hall number. . . .

Christy Brown, Down All the Days

7. Nick's heart, /, swelled with sweet thoughts of his wife and child, who lived in a foreign city across an ocean.

Edmund Ware, "An Underground Episode"

8. (Contains two.) And he, /, at once looked over his shoulder at her and, /, signaled that he would meet her.

Theodore Dreiser, An American Tragedy

Practice 8

For each of the sentences below, provide three different expansions, as in the example. For each expansion, try to vary not only the content but also the structure or combination of structures used in the subject-verb split. Also, vary the length: some short, some medium, some long. Punctuate correctly. Compare your sentences with the originals in the References on pages 185–186.

Example

Reduced Sentence

That night after supper Mr. Delahanty, /, said to his wife, "I think I'll just stay home and read tonight."

Sample Expansions

a. That night after supper Mr. Delahanty, **needing a night off from party going and social obligations to get ready for his C.P.A. test**, said to his wife, "I think I'll just stay home and read tonight."

b. That night after supper Mr. Delahanty, **who was nursing a grudge against his wife caused by what he considered her excessive gallivanting**, said, "I think I'll just stay home and read tonight."

c. That night after supper Mr. Delahanty, **the classic example of the homebody type husband who prefers to avoid the discomforts of social occasions**, said to his wife, "I think I'll just stay home and read tonight."

Original Sentence

That night after supper Mr. Delahanty, **who had been up at five, irrigating, and who was put out with a climate so tardy with its rains that irrigating this late in November was necessary**, said to his wife, "I think I'll just stay home and read tonight."

Jessamyn West, "Cress Delahanty"

1. The Irish, / , stripped before battle and rushed their enemy naked, carrying sword and shield but wearing only sandals . . . .

Thomas Cahill, How the Irish Saved Civilization

2. Once Enoch Bentley, /, struck his father, old Tom Bentley, with the butt of a teamster's whip, and the old man seemed likely to die.

Sherwood Anderson, Winesburg, Ohio

3. McCaslin, /, watched until the other's shadow sank down the wall and vanished, becoming one with the mass of sleeping shadows.

William Faulkner, "Delta Autumn"

4. The big hands, /, hang loose off the wrist bone like clumsy, homemade tools hung on the wall of a shed.

Robert Penn Warren, "The Patented Gate and the Mean Hamburger"

5. (Contains two.) And Clyde, /, had not the courage or persistence or the background to go further with her now, went for his coat, and, /, departed.

Theodore Dreiser, An American Tragedy

Practice 9

From a recent piece of writing of your own, select five sentences that don't have subject-verb splits. Add them.

*F*ocus 12

Sentence Closers

Here's a list of sentences, all written by professional writers, but with some parts deleted.

1. It ran.

2. He strode forward.

3. He hung around L.A.

4. By and by, one group after another came straggling back to the mouth of the cave.

5. I would huddle.

Now compare the sentences above with the originals below. Notice that it's the **boldface** parts (sentence closers) that account for the professional sentence variety.

1a.   It ran, **its pelvic bones crushing aside trees and bushes, its taloned feet clawing damp earth, leaving prints six inches deep wherever it settled its weight**.
Ray Bradbury, "A Sound of Thunder"

2a.   He strode forward, **crushing ants with each step, and brushing them off his clothes, till he stood above the skeleton, which lay sprawled under a small bush**.
Doris Lessing, "A Sunrise on the Veld" from African Stories

3a.   He hung around L.A., **broke most of the time, working as an usher in movie theatres, getting an occasional part as an extra on the lots, or a bit on TV, dreaming and yearning and hungry, eating cold spaghetti out of the can**.
John Dos Passos, "The Sinister Adolescents"

4a.   By and by, one group after another came straggling back to the mouth of the cave, **panting, hilarious, smeared from head to foot with tallow drippings, daubed with clay, and entirely delighted with the success of the day**.
Mark Twain, The Adventures of Tom Sawyer

5a. I would huddle, **listening to their noise in the darkness,
my eyebrows lifted, my lips pursed, the hair on the
back of my neck standing up like pigs' bristle**.

John Gardner, Grendel

Definition of a Sentence Closer

A sentence closer is any structure that occupies the closing
position of a sentence. Here are examples:

1. She often spoke of her life there, **living in luxury amidst
plantations, servants, and saddle horses**.

Charlie Chaplin, My Autobiography

2. He carries a banana, **which he keeps offering to the bird,
who just squawks and spits blood at him**.

Frank McCourt, Angela's Ashes

3. She returned to her bench, **her face showing all the
unhappiness that had suddenly overtaken her**.

Theodore Dreiser, An American Tragedy

4. Bailey had graduated the year before, **although to do so he
had had to forfeit all pleasures to make up for his time
lost in Baton Rouge**.

Maya Angelou, I Know Why the Caged Bird Sings

5. He must conquer the snow, **this new, white brute force
which had accumulated against him**.

D. H. Lawrence, "The Man Who Loved Islands"

Practice 1

Unscramble the sentence parts to produce a sentence with a
sentence closer. Some sentences have more than one sentence
closer; for those, decide the best order. Punctuate correctly, with
one comma before each sentence closer. Compare your results
with the originals in the References on page 186.

1a. limping

 b. he went on

William Faulkner, "Dry September"

2a. for what reason neither grand-parent would tell

  b. from Grandpa

  c. she was separated
                    Charlie Chaplin, My Autobiography

3a. not rolling

  b. it was a heavy sound

  c. hard and sharp
                         Theodore Taylor, The Cay

4a. trying to be together as long as possible

  b. and so we went to the station, across the meadow

  c. taking the longer way
                    Gerda Weissmann Klein, All But My Life

5a. and even changing the well-known scents

  b. filling the whole room

  c. sometimes a gaggle of them came to the store

  d. chasing out the air
                Maya Angelou, I Know Why the Caged Bird Sings

6a. a shadow

  b. hour after hour

  c. motionless

  d. he stood there silent

  e. carved in ebony and moonlight
                         James V. Marshall, Walkabout

7a. a gigantic race

  b. before the creation

  c. Prometheus was one of the Titans

  d. who inhabited the earth

  e. of man
                Thomas Bulfinch, "Prometheus and Pandora"

8a. light flickered on bits of ruby glass

b. and on sensitive capillary hairs

c. in the nylon-brushed nostrils

d. on rubber-padded paws

e. its eight legs spidered under it

f. of the creature that quivered gently, gently

Ray Bradbury, Fahrenheit 451

Practice 2

Identify any structures that could become sentence closers and rearrange each sentence so that it has a sentence closer. Compare yours with the originals in the References on pages 186–187.

Scrambled Sentences

1. Buck, the successful champion, the dominant primordial beast who had made his kill and found it good, stood and looked on.

Jack London, The Call of the Wild

2. Hunched up under the blankets now, utterly relaxed, the Arab, his mouth open, was asleep.

Albert Camus, "The Guest"

3. Buying furniture on the installment plan, being cheated and yet knowing no way to avoid it, that winter my mother and brother came, and we set up housekeeping.

Richard Wright, Black Boy

4. Running hard, their heads down, their forearms working, their breath whistling, six boys, half an hour early that afternoon, came over the hill.

John Steinbeck, The Red Pony

5. Somewhere, high above me, like some goddess whom I had discovered and regarded as my very own, she was always up there.

Henry Miller, Stand Still Like the Hummingbird

6. On the stone floor of the pantry, face down, arms twisted at a
   curious angle, clad just in his vest and trousers, feet bare,
   Father lay crumped up.

   Christy Brown, Down All the Days

Practice 3

Unscramble each sentence to produce a sentence similar in
structure to the model. The model sentence contains four
sentence closers, three short, and one (the last) somewhat
longer. Compare yours with the ones in the References on page
187.

> Model: I would huddle, **listening to their noise in the
> darkness, my eyebrows lifted, my lips pursed, the hair on
> the back of my neck standing up like pigs' bristle**.
>
> *John Gardner*, Grendel

Scrambled Imitations

1a. deciding about their agenda for the sales meeting

 b. they would meet

 c. their opinions uncertain

 d. the leader of the group of section chiefs shouting out like a
    huckster

 e. their interest high

2a. their stems poised

 b. she smiled

 c. the arrangement of the bouquet of roses looking like a
    prizewinner

 d. their blossoms in full bloom

 e. glancing at the flowers in the vase

Practice 4

Combine the list into one sentence having basically the same sentence structure as the model. Compare yours with the ones in the References on pages 187–188. Finally, write an imitation of the model with the same structure as the model but your own content.

Example

Model: Before she could put a stop to it, some of their classmates scoffed at the leaf-lard-and-black-bread sandwiches they ate for lunch, **huddled in one corner of the recreation room, dressed in their boiled-out ragpickers' clothes**.

Ambrose Flack, "The Strangers That Came to Town"

Sentences to Be Combined

a. Something happened when he selected a color for the sky.

b. One of his teachers commented on the bright hue.

c. The bright hue was the one he chose for backgrounds.

d. The bright hue was chosen with an aim.

e. The aim was toward a bold creativity.

f. The bright hue was applied.

g. The manner of application was with his most flamboyant brush strokes.

Combination

When he selected a color for the sky, one of his teachers commented on the bright hue he chose for backgrounds, **chosen with an aim toward a bold creativity, applied with his most flamboyant brush strokes**.

Imitation

If the borrower damaged the cover of the book, several of the librarians complained about the scant concern borrowers gave to proper care, **governed only by their desire for enjoyment, unconcerned about their selfish carelessness**.

1. Model: Close to the village there lived a lady, **a small landowner who had an estate of about three hundred acres**.

   Leo Tolstoy, "How Much Land Does a Man Need?"

   a. This occurred high up the tree.

   b. There climbed some girls.

   c. They were little adventurers.

   d. They were ones who imagined a great escapade.

   e. The escapade was of nearly Everest proportions.

2. Model: Touching the ropes and knots which joined the raft together, he stooped down, **his arms and shoulders buried under the cold water, and his chin kissing the rippling surface of the river**.

   Shen T'Sung Wen, "Under Cover of Darkness," translated by Y. Chia-Hua and Robert Payne

   a. He was inspecting the plumbing and fixtures.

   b. The plumbing and fixtures outfitted the new bathroom.

   c. He walked around.

   d. His tappings and probings were done.

   e. They were done with his expert skill.

   f. In addition, his experience was guiding his assessment.

   g. The assessment was of the work.

3. Model: I could see the string of camels bearing the merchandise, and the company of turbaned merchants, **carrying some of their queer old firearms, and some of their spears, journeying downward toward the plains**.

   Sir Rabindranath Tagore, "The Cabuliwallah"

   a. They could foresee a time.

   b. The time was of soldiers ending their battles.

   c. They could foresee, in addition, a period of permanent truce.

   d. They would be negotiating their disputes.

e. The disputes were about politics.

f. The disputes were about, in addition, many of the old arguments.

g. They would be living peacefully within dissent.

4. Model: Now it is night, and I am wrapped in a traveling rug on top of a four-in-hand coach, **driving with Mother and theatrical friends, cosseted in their gaiety and laughter as our trumpeter, with clarion braggadocio, heralds us along the Kennington Road to the rhythmic jingle of harness and the beat of horses' hoofs**.

Charlie Chaplin, My Autobiography

a. Then it was graduation.

b. In addition, they were encouraged by a dream.

c. The dream was of new beginnings.

d. The new beginnings were for their lives.

e. They were marching among friends and proud parents.

f. They were dressed in their caps and gowns.

g. This all happened as the orchestra stirred them.

h. It stirred them with lusty fanfares.

i. It stirred them with its majesty of the pomp of trumpet blares.

j. It stirred them, in addition, with the circumstances of the formal rite of passage.

Practice 5

Following the structure of the model sentence, but using your own content, write a sentence imitation of each of the models below. Imitate the structure of the entire sentence, not just the sentence closer.

1. Finally the train drew in, **a large shining iron monster puffing smoke**.

Margaret Atwood, Alias Grace

2. The children crawled over the shelves and into the potato and onion bins, **twanging all the time in their sharp voices like cigar-box guitars**.
   Maya Angelou, I Know Why the Caged Bird Sings

3. I enjoyed going to the shop, **even though we had to assemble and march out of the ghetto under guard, and be counted like cattle at departure and arrival**.
   Gerda Weissmann Klein, All But My Life

4. It had a black spot on it, **the black spot Mr. Summers had made the night before with heavy pencil in the coal-company office**.
   Shirley Jackson, "The Lottery"

5. As he ran away into the darkness, they repented of their weakness and ran after him, **swearing** and **throwing sticks and great balls of soft mud at the figure that screamed and ran faster and faster into the darkness**.
   Sherwood Anderson, Winesburg, Ohio

6. The strength that had been as a miracle in her body left, and she half reeled across the floor, **clutching at the back of the chair in which she had spent so many long days staring out over the tin roofs into the main street of Winesburg**.
   Sherwood Anderson, Winesburg, Ohio

Practice 6

Change the sentences underneath into the first sentence into sentence closers to insert at the slash mark. Compare your sentences with the originals in the References on page 188. After you have combined the sentences into one, write an imitation of the resulting sentence with your own content but the structure of the model.

Example

a. It was falling on every part of the dark central plain, /, /, /, /.

b. It was falling on the treeless hills.

c. It was falling softly upon the Bog of Allen.

d. In addition, it was falling farther westward.

e. It was softly falling into the dark mutinous Shannon waves.

Combination with Sentence Closers

It was falling on every part of the dark central plain, **on the treeless hills, falling softly upon the Bog of Allen and, farther westward, softly falling into the dark mutinous Shannon waves**.

James Joyce, "The Dead"

Imitation

They were playing at various concerts of rock and roll, **at jammed theatres, entertaining powerfully in America and, even abroad, powerfully entertaining in sold-out European public halls**.

1a. I seemed forever condemned, /.

 b. I was ringed by walls.

From *Richard Wright*, Black Boy

2a. I waited for Andries at the back of the queue, /.

 b. I was out of the reach of the white man's mocking eyes.

From *Peter Abrahams*, Tell Freedom

3a. The Fog Horn was blowing steadily, /.

 b. It was blowing once every fifteen seconds.

From *Ray Bradbury, "The Fog Horn"*

4a. Gradually his head began to revolve, /, /.

 b. It revolved slowly.

 c. It revolved rhythmically.

From *D. H. Lawrence, "The Prussian Officer"*

5a. Down on the little landing-bay were three cottages in a row, /,

 b. The cottages were like coast guards' cottages.

 c. The cottages were all neat and whitewashed.

From *D. H. Lawrence,
"The Man Who Loved Islands"*

6a.   He spent long, silent hours in his study, /, /, /.

b.   He was working not very fast.

c.   Nor was he working very importantly.

d.   He was letting the writing spin softly from him as if it were drowsy gossamer.

From *D. H. Lawrence,*
"The Man Who Loved Islands"

Practice 7

Combine each list of sentences into one sentence containing a sentence closer(s). You may eliminate words, or change their form, so long as the intended meaning remains. Punctuate correctly. Compare your work with the originals in the References on pages 188–189.

1a.   The little boy stared at Ferris.

b.   The little boy was amazed.

c.   The little boy was, in addition, unbelieving.

From *Carson McCullers, "The Sojourner"*

2a.   I came out crawling.

b.   I was clinging to the handle of the door.

c.   I did all of this until I made sure of my bearings.

From *Richard E. Byrd,* Alone

3a.   Nick fought him.

b.   The fighting was against the current.

c.   Nick was letting him thump in the water.

d.   The thumping in the water was against the spring.

e.   The spring was of the rod.

From *Ernest Hemingway,*
"Big Two-Hearted River: Part II"

4a.   Hattie sat down.

b.   She sat at her old Spanish table.

  c. She was watching them in the cloudy warmth of the day.

  d. She was clasping her hands.

  e. She was chuckling and sad.

From *Saul Bellow,*
"Leaving the Yellow House"

5a. Nick climbed out onto the meadow.

  b. In addition, he stood.

  c. Water was running down his trousers.

  d. Water was running, in addition, out of his shoes.

  e. His shoes were squlchy.

From *Ernest Hemingway,*
"Big Two-Hearted River: Part II"

6a. He walked with a prim strut.

  b. He was swinging out his legs.

  c. He swung them in a half-circle with each step.

  d. His heels were biting smartly.

  e. The biting was into the carpet.

  f. The carpet was red velvet.

  g. The carpet was on the floor.

From *Carson McCullers, "The Jockey"*

7a. The old woman slid to the edge.

  b. The edge was of her chair.

  c. In addition, she leaned.

  d. The leaning was forward.

  e. She was shading her eyes from the sunset.

  f. The sunset was piercing.

  g. She was shading her eyes with her hand.

From *Flannery O'Connor,*
"The Life You Save May Be Your Own"

Note: The sentence below contains sentence closers at the end of each of the two main clauses in the sentence.

8a.   The horse galloped along wearily.

b.   The galloping was under the morning sky.

c.   The sky was murky.

d.   The horse was dragging his old rattling box after his heels.

e.   In addition, Gabriel was again in a cab with her.

f.   They were galloping to catch the boat.

g.   They were galloping to their honeymoon.

From *James Joyce, "The Dead"*

Practice 8

Add sentence closers to each of the reduced sentences below. Each of the sentences, in their original complete versions, has sentence closers in the places indicated by slash marks. Compare your sentences with the originals in the References on page 189.

Example

Reduced Sentence

We groped in the ruins and came upon this, and there he was, /, /, /.

Student-Expanded Sentence

We groped in the ruins and came upon this, and there he was, **a man about sixty, his clothes so neat that his attire contradicted his surroundings, a place for a gathering of derelicts**.

Original Sentence

We groped in the ruins and came upon this, and there he was, **sitting in his bunk, surrounded by foam and wreckage, jabbering cheerfully to himself**.

Joseph Conrad, "Youth"

---

1. She stood out from all the other girls in the school, /.
   Henry Miller, Stand Still Like the Hummingbird

2. His face was fleshy and pallid, /.
   James Joyce, "The Dead"

3. Todd's hands were clenched into fists, / .
   Stephen King, "Apt Pupil"

4. His earnestness affected the boy, /.
   Sherwood Anderson, Winesburg, Ohio

5. Ian appeared at the back door, / .
   Anne Tyler, Saint Maybe

6. Mary Jane gazed after her, /, /.
   James Joyce, "The Dead"

7. As far down the long stretch as he could see, the trout were rising, /, /.
   Ernest Hemingway, "Big Two-Hearted River: Part I"

8. The girl at first did not return any of the kisses, but presently she began to, and after she had put several on his cheek, she reached his lips and remained there, /.
   Flannery O'Connor, "Good Country People"

Practice 9

From a recent piece of writing of your own, select five sentences that don't have sentence closers. Add them.

*F*ocus 13

Reviewing the Positions

When you buy a new car, it's the additions—options and accessories—that make the car better, more desirable, more valuable. The same is true with sentences: additions produce better sentences—more like those of the pros—"souped-up, not stripped down." This final review provides practice adding sentence parts to create powerful sentences.

Practice 1

Below are stripped-down sentences, with the sentence parts from the original sentences underneath. In the original sentences, those parts occupied *two different positions*—openers, subject-verb splits, closers. Soup-up each sentence by adding the sentence parts in *two different positions*. Compare your sentences with the originals on pages 189–196 in the References.

1. The grass was high.

    a. around the old gravestones

    b. untended

    > *E. L. Doctorow*, The Waterworks

2. The sled went over.

    a. as they swung on the turn

    b. spilling half its load through the loose lashings
    > *Jack London*, The Call of the Wild

3. Snow White saw the faces of seven bearded, vertically challenged men.

    a. when she awoke several hours later

    b. surrounding the bed
    > *James Finn Garner*, Politically Correct Bedtime Stories

4. Fletcher Seagull conquered his sixteen-point vertical slow roll and the next day topped it off with a triple cartwheel.

a. who loved aerobatics like no one else

b. his feathers flashing white sunlight to a beach from which more than one furtive eye watched
Richard Bach, Jonathan Livingston Seagull

5. I fixed my attention upon Reverend Sykes.

   a. subdued

   b. who seemed to be waiting for me to settle down
   Harper Lee, To Kill a Mockingbird

6. Alfred bolted across the street.

   a. wildly

   b. sidestepping a taxicab by inches

   c. ignoring the horns and curses of braking drivers
   Robert Lipsyte, The Contender

7. The man was still asleep.

   a. in the far corner

   b. snoring slightly on the intaking breath

   c. his head back against the wall
   Ernest Hemingway, "The Undefeated"

8. She looked at the bright stars.

   a. at night

   b. sleeping little

   c. listening to the river
   Larry McMurtry, Streets of Laredo

9. A big kitchen table was neatly set as if for a big party.

   a. covered with one of those old-fashioned oilcloths

   b. with eight chairs

   c. two on each side of the table
   Robert Cormier, Take Me Where the Good Times Are

10. Caroline received uniformly high grades.

     a. an excellent student

     b. which she worked hard to get

     c. doing more than two hours of homework each day
          Lester David, Jacqueline Kennedy Onassis

11. My brothers and I buried mother.

     a. at the cemetery

     b. taking our time speaking to her

     c. as though she could hear us
          Pat Conroy, Beach Music

12. Across the open hearth sat my father.

     a. his face lit by flames

     b. leaning forward

     c. his hands outspread to his knees

     d. his shoulders tense
          Christy Brown, My Left Foot

13. A structure appeared.

     a. beyond the driver

     b. beyond the windshield

     c. indistinct

     d. unidentifiable
          Dean Koontz, Intensity

14. I saw Viola in her black dress.

     a. across the tops

     b. of about a hundred gravestones and many people

     c. standing on a little rise

     d. her gray hair wandering from its knot
          Barbara Kingsolver, Animal Dreams

15. A young American mother sat on the edge of a steel-framed bed.

a. in an upstairs bedroom

b. shortly

c. before dawn

d. rocking her nursing daughter

Steve Estes, Called to Die

16. Wheelchair vans or ambulances or private cars parked in front of the portico, and new residents were escorted in.

a. periodically

b. a few on their own feet

c. others in wheelchairs

d. some on gurneys

Tracy Kidder, Old Friends

17. Roland has stopped chopping and is sitting on the chopping block.

a. outside the window

b. his arms on his knees

c. his big hands dangling

d. staring off into the trees

Margaret Atwood, Wilderness Tips

18. The river Rhine froze solid.

a. On the last, cold day

b. of December

c. in the year 406

d. providing the natural bridge the hundreds of thousands of hungry men, women, and children had been waiting for

Thomas Cahill, How the Irish Saved Civilization

19. He had seemed of no more than medium height.

a. at the university

b. in his gray suit

    c. perhaps because he stooped so attentively to hear the slightest word from the person he was talking to

    d. perhaps because his neat, fair hair made him look somehow ineffectual

Wallace Stegner, Crossing to Safety

20. He came up to the house again and said good-bye to the children.

    a. at three forty-five

    b. who were seated on the porch

    c. drinking apple juice and

    d. eating graham crackers and

    e. rolling pebbles back and forth

David Guterson, Snow Falling on Cedars

21. The streets turn from the thickest dust into the direst mud.

    a. after rain or

    b. when snowfalls thaw

    c. unnamed

    d. unshaded

    e. unpaved

Truman Capote, In Cold Blood

22. He washed his hand in the ocean and held it there for more than a minute.

    a. shifting the weight of the line to his shoulder and

    b. kneeling carefully

    c. submerged

    d. watching the blood trail away and the steady movement of the water against his hand

    e. as the boat moved

Ernest Hemingway, The Old Man and the Sea

23. Waves washed perilously close to the lighthouse.

    a. on occasions

    b. when the tide ran exceptionally high

    c. dashing its base

    d. with salt-tinged algae

    e. which clung to it now like a sea moss
            David Guterson, Snow Falling on Cedars

24. He moved.

    a. turning

    b. his shoulder pressing against the wall

    c. until he was standing sideways

    d. his feet together on the narrow ledge

    e. his side hugging the wall

    f. as he faced the wide opening
            Robb White, Deathwatch

25. His right hand flew over the ledge.

    a. blindly

    b. his fingers dancing across it

    c. reaching

    d. feeling

    e. searching

    f. until his body began to drop
            Robb White, Deathwatch

26. Quoyle went to the wharf on his way to Wavey.

    a. in the morning

    b. breakfastless and

    c. shaky

    d. from seven cups

e. of coffee

f. heart and stomach aching
   E. Annie Proulx, The Shipping News

27. Lived a family of bears.

    a. through the thicket

    b. across the river, and

    c. in the deep, deep woods

    d. a Papa bear

    e. a Mama Bear and

    f. a Baby Bear

    g. who all lived together anthropomorphically in a little cottage as a nuclear family
       James Finn Garner, Politically Correct Bedtime Stories

28. She was sent to sleep.

    a. when Laurel was a child

    b. by the beloved reading voice

    c. under a velvety cloak

    d. of words

    e. patterned richly and

    f. stitched with gold

    g. coming straight out

    h. of a fairy tale

    i. while the voice went on reading aloud into her dreams
       Eudora Welty, The Optimist's Daughter

29. The sun began to sink.

    a. red and

    b. enormous

    c. into the western sky

    d. the moon beginning to rise

e. on the other side

f. of the river

g. with its own glorious shade

h. of red

i. coming up out of the trees like a russet firebird
   Pat Conroy, The Prince of Tides

30. My eyes roamed.

a. in the half-light

b. around my room

c. a cramped space

d. the room of an only child

e. tidy

f. organized completely

g. with the possessory feel

h. of everything

i. in place

j. unmolested by any of the brothers and sisters I had for
   years longed to have and now, in my desolation, longed
   for with a special ache
   William Styron, A Tidewater Morning

The Last Practice

Add an opener, a subject-verb split, and a closer to each
sentence in the paragraphs below. Write paragraphs that
clearly prove you've accomplished the goal of this worktext:
composing sentences resembling those of professional
writers.

First you have to learn something, and then you can go out and
do it.

Mies van der Rohe

Paragraph 1: *The Detective*

(1) The detective found only one clue. (2) His partner stood over the body. (3) A crime lab professional worked around them. (4) A single bystander watched everything.

Paragraph 2: *The Doctor*

(1) The doctor prepared for surgery. (2) Her assistant was nearby. (3) The anesthesiologist stood ready. (4) The patient lay on the operating table.

Paragraph 3: *The Student*

(1) The student stared at the test. (2) The teacher stood in the front of the room. (3) The class was quiet. (4) The test was challenging.

Paragraph 4: *The Professional Writer—YOU!*

(1) [Your name] picked up a pen. (2) [He/she] thought for a minute. (3) [He/she] began to write. (4) The sentence was a dazzler!

Paragraph 5: *Your Choice*

Write your own four-sentence paragraph that includes in every sentence an opener, an subject-verb split, and a closer.

References

Focus 1
Sentence Unscrambling

Practice 1 (pages 3–6)
1. He ran from the place, leaving his suitcase, leaving the quirt, leaving the oak box of money.

2. The father was respectable and tight, a mortgage financier and a stern, upright collection-plate passer and forecloser.

3. After Buck Fanshaw's inquest, a meeting of the short-haired brotherhood was held, for nothing can be done on the Pacific coast without a public meeting and an expression of sentiment.

4. With them, carrying a gnarled walking stick, was Elmo Goodhue Pipgrass, the littlest, oldest man I had ever seen.

5. He bounded out of bed wearing a long flannel nightgown over long woolen underwear, a nightcap, and a leather jacket around his chest.

6. Once upon a sunny morning a man who sat in a breakfast nook looked up from his scrambled eggs to see a white unicorn with a gold horn quietly cropping the roses in the garden.

7. Then, out of a box on the bed, she removed the gleaming pair of patent-leather dancing pumps, grabbed my right foot, and shoved it into one of them, using her finger as a shoehorn.

Practice 2 (pages 6–8)
Part One: Then it moved around the side of the car. The big raised tail blocked their view out of all the side windows. At the back the

animal snorted, a deep rumbling growl that blended with the thunder. It sank its jaws into the spare tire mounted on the back of the Land Cruiser and, in a single head shake, tore it away. The rear of the car lifted into the air for a moment, and then it thumped down with a muddy splash.

Part Two: As if in the superhuman energy of his utterance there had been found the potency of a spell, the huge antique panels to which the speaker pointed threw slowly back, upon the instant, their ponderous and ebony jaws. It was the work of the rushing gust—but then without those doors there did stand the lofty and enshrouded figure of the Lady Madeline of Usher. There was blood upon her white robes, and the evidence of some bitter struggle upon every portion of her emaciated frame. For a moment she remained trembling and reeling to and fro upon the threshold—then, with a low, moaning cry, fell heavily inward upon the person of her brother, and in her violent and now final death-agonies, bore him to the floor a corpse, and a victim to the the terrors he had anticipated.

Practice 3
Answers will vary.

Practice 4
Answers will vary.

Focus 2
Sentence Imitating

Practice 1 (pages 11–13)
1. Different: b

Sources

    a. *Jack London, "All Gold Cañon"*

    b. *Tate, "Ghost Men of Coronado"*

c. *Don Killgallon*

2. Different: b

Sources

a. *Bernard Malamud*, The Assistant

b. *Ernest Hemingway*, Green Hills of Africa

c. *Don Killgallon*

3. Different: b

Sources

a. *Don Killgallon*

b. *Henry G. Felsen, "Horatio"*

c. *John Steinbeck, "Flight"*

4. Different: c

Sources

a. *Don Killgallon*

b. *Joseph Conrad, "The Idiots"*

c. *William Faulkner*, Intruder in the Dust

5. Different: b

Sources

a. *Don Killgallon*

b. *Ray Bradbury*, Fahrenheit 451

c. *Aldous Huxley*, Antic Hay

6. Different: a

Sources

a. *Ernest Hemingway*, For Whom the Bell Tolls

b. *Don Killgallon*

c. *John Hersey*, Hiroshima

Focus 3
Sentence Combining

Practice 2 (pages 24–26)

1. The boy watched, his eyes bulging in the dark.

2. One of the dogs, the best one, had disappeared.

3. Jumping to his feet and breaking off the tale, Doctor Parcival began to walk up and down in the office of the *Winesburg Eagle* where George Willard sat listening.

4. This land was waterless, furred with the cacti which could store water and with the great-rooted brush which could reach deep into the earth for a little moisture and get along on very little.

5. It glided through, brushing the overhanging twigs, and disappeared from the river like some slim and amphibious creature leaving the water for its lair in the forests.

Practice 3 (pages 26–27)

1. The country house, on this particular wintry afternoon, was most enjoyable.

2. The sun was setting when the truck came back, and the earth was bloody in its setting light.

3. He moves nervously and fast, but with a restraint that suggests that he is a cautious, thoughtful man.

4. The girls stood aside, talking among themselves, looking over their shoulders at the boys, and the very small children rolled in the dust or clung to the hands of their older brothers or sisters.

5. He took flour and oil, shaped a cake in a frying pan, and lighted the little stove that functioned on bottled gas.

Practice 4 (pages 27–29)

1. From ten to fifteen he distributed handbills for merchants, held horses, and ran confidential errands.

2. Nick looked down into clear, brown water, colored from the pebbly bottom, and watched the trout keeping themselves steady in the current with wavering fins.

3. On one side, beginning at the very lip of the pool, was a tiny meadow, a cool, resilient surface of green that extended to the base of the browning wall.

4. In the stillness of the air every tree, every leaf, every bough, every tendril of creeper and every petal of minute blossoms seemed to have been bewitched into an immobility perfect and final.

Practice 5 (pages 29–32)
Paragraph 1

(1) Manuel, leaning against the barrera, watching the bull, waved his hand, and the gypsy ran out, trailing his cape. (2) The bull, in full gallop, pivoted and charged the cape, his head down, his tail rising. (3) The gypsy moved in a zigzag, and as he passed, the bull caught sight of him and abandoned the cape to charge the man. (4) The gypsy sprinted and vaulted the red fence of the barrera as the bull struck it with his horns. (5) He tossed into it twice with his horns, banging into the wood blindly.

Paragraph 2

(1) To have a dance, the women sit in a circle with their babies asleep on their backs and sing medicine songs in several parts with falsetto voices, clapping their hands in a sharp, staccato rhythm at counterpoint to the rhythm of their voices. (2) Behind their backs the men dance one behind the other, circling slowly around, taking very short, pounding steps which are again at counterpoint to both the rhythms of the singing and the clapping. (3) Now and then the men sing, too, in their deeper voices, and their dance rattles—rattles made from dry cocoons strung together with sinew cords and tied to their legs—add a sharp, high clatter like the sound of shaken gourds, very well timed because the men step accurately. (4) A Bushman dance is an infinitely complicated pattern of voices and rhythm, an orchestra of bodies, making music that is infinitely varied and always precise.

Practice 6 (pages 32–35)
Paragraph 1

(1) Outside, upon this lawn, stood an iron deer. (2) Further up on the green stood a tall brown Victorian house, quiet in the sunlight, all covered with scrolls and rococo, its windows made of blue and pink and yellow and green colored glass. (3) Upon the porch were hairy geraniums and an old swing which was hooked into the porch ceiling and which now swung back and forth, back and forth, in a little breeze. (4) At the summit of the house was a cupola with diamond leaded-glass windows and a dunce-cap roof!

Paragraph 2

(1) Upon the half decayed veranda of a small frame house that stood near the edge of a ravine near the town of Winesburg, Ohio, a fat little old man walked nervously up and down. (2) Across a long field that had been seeded for clover but that had produced only a dense crop of yellow mustard weeds, he could see the public highway along which went a wagon filled with berry pickers returning from the fields. (3) The berry pickers, youths and maidens, laughed and shouted boisterously. (4) A boy clad in a blue shirt leaped from the wagon and attempted to drag after him one of the maidens who screamed and protested shrilly. (5) The feet of the boy in the road kicked up a cloud of dust that floated across the face of the departing sun.

Focus 4
Sentence Expanding

Practice 2 (pages 38–39)

1. She sprang dynamically to her feet, **clinching her hands**, then swiftly and noiselessly crossed over to her bed and, **from underneath it**, dragged out her suitcase.

2. He stood there, **rubbing his injured shoulder**, and Rainsford, **with fear again gripping his heart**, heard the general's mocking laugh ring through the jungle.

3. **Five, six, eight times**, he knocked the big man down, and the big man came again, **staggering, slavering, raving, vainly trying to rend and smash**.

4. We spent several evenings together, and the last one was the funniest, **because this time Joyce, who always had quite a lot to drink, got really potted**.

5. That night in the south upstairs chamber, **a hot little room where a full-leaded chinaberry tree shut all the air from the single window**, Emmett lay in a kind of trance.

6. **With something of the childish belief in miracles with which he had so often gone to class, all his lessons unlearned**, Paul dressed and dashed whistling down the corridor to the elevator.

Practice 3 (page 39)
1. **I sat in their room**, helping her get ready, uttering cheerful banalities, and, at the same time, wondering how she felt as she looked in the mirror and saw the partially paralyzed cheek, the deepened lines, the wrinkled skin that hung down from her upper arms.

2. On the outskirts of town, **she came upon her destination**, though at first she did not realize it.

3. **He stirred and drank it down**, sweet, hot, and warming his empty stomach.

4. When the hostess saw that I was awake and that my safety belt was already fastened, **she smiled efficiently and moved on down the aisle**, waking the other passengers and asking them to fasten their safety belts.

5. Running up the street with all his might, **Marty could see that the game would start any minute now**.

6. At night, untired after the day's work, **he washed first in turpentine and then in water, and talked with the family**.

Practice 4 (pages 39–40)
1. In the hall stood an enormous truck, **behind the ladder that led to the roof, just opposite Hedger's door**.

2. All members of the staff, **from the ornithologists and researchers to the girls in the bookstore**, wore plastic tags bearing their names and color photographs.

3. Jerry stood on the landing, **smiling nervously**.

4. They lived in a square two-flat house tightly packed among identical houses on a fog-enveloped street in the Sunset district of San Francisco, **less than a mile from the ocean, more than three miles from Nob Hill, more than three thousand miles from Times Square**.

5. His teeth, **while strong and sharp**, were, **as weapons of offense**, pitifully inadequate by comparison with the mighty fighting fangs of the anthropoids.

6. **In the long, burning, murmurous Virginia summers**, he used to ride, **alone, back into the country towards the mountains, along the clay roads, dusty and red, and through the sweet-scented long grasses of the fields**.

7. **With an exclamation**, she tossed her book to the deck, **where it sprawled at a straddle**, and hurried to the rail.

8. **When one half of the world is angry at the other half, or one half of a nation is angry at the rest, or one side of town feuds with the other side**, it is hardly surprising, **when you stop to think about it**, that so many people lose their tempers with so many other people.

Practice 5 (pages 40–41)

1. **Standing in an aisle in a library**, he can feel the eyes on him.

2. She made the best meatloaf in the world, **and would give it to me raw, seasoned with onions and green peppers, from the bowl**.

3. **Now, lying in the ditch with Billy and the scouts after having been shot at**, Weary made Billy take a very close look at his trench knife.

4. **In the monastery where they stayed, Parador de San Francisco**, the gardens were laid out so neatly, **with fountains and stone benches, and stones inlaid on the walkways**.

5. **Above the open shirt**, a pale silk scarf is tied around his neck, **almost completely hiding from view the throat whose creases are the only sign of his age**.

6. **After this climax**, the four animals continued to lead their lives, **so rudely broken in upon by civil war, in great joy and contentment, undisturbed by further risings or invasions**.

7. He went into the kitchen, **where the moonlight called his attention to a half bottle of champagne on the kitchen table, all that was left from the reception in the tent**.

Focus 5
Reviewing the Techniques

Practices 1–3 (pages 42–47)
Answers will vary.

Practice 4 (pages 47–48)

1. **Upon a stage**, a woman sang.

2. A large woman, **wearing faded overalls**, got out and waddled over to them.

3. Mary asked no more questions but waited in the darkness of her corner, **keeping her eyes on the window**.

4. **Crumpled there**, he held his temples desperately with both hands and was wretchedly sick.

5. He walked on, **surrounded by skipping, laughing children**.

6. **Around the fiery circle**, warriors on high stilts beat upraised swords against their shields.

7. Ima Dean, with a huge bag of yellow and red wrapped candies, was sitting on the floor, **delving into it, making one big pile and three smaller ones**.

8. He was a broad, brandy-legged little man with a walrus mustache, with square hands, **puffed and muscled on the palms**.

9. They were standing there in front of the locked door in the nearly empty plane, **laughing wildly**, when the man in the

red shirt and the man in the crew-necked jersey arrived, **looking at them as if they had both gone crazy**.

10. **Across the stalk land, into the pine woods, into the climbing, brightening glow of the dawn**, the boy followed the dog, **whose anxious pace slowed from age as they went**.

Focus 6
Absolute Phrase

Practice 1 (pages 53–54)

1. High in the air, a little figure, **his hands thrust in his short jacket pockets**, stood staring out to sea. (subject-verb split)

2. He walked with a prim strut, swinging out his legs in a half-circle with each step, **his heels biting smartly into the red velvet carpet on the floor**. (sentence closer)

3. Outside, **his carpetbag in his hand**, he stood for a time in the barnyard. (sentence opener)

4. Father lay crumped up on the stone floor of the pantry, **[his] face down, [his] arms twisted at a curious angle. . . .** (sentence closers, with the possessive pronoun *his* implied in each)

Practice 2 (pages 54–55)

1. I was awake for quite a long time, thinking about things and watching Catherine sleeping, **the moonlight on her face**.

2. One of many small groups of children, **each child carrying his little bag of crackling**, we trod the long road home in the cold winter afternoon.

3. I looked across to a lighted case of Chinese design which held delicate-looking statues of horses and birds, small vases and bowls, **each set upon a carved wooden base**.

Practice 3 (pages 55–56)

1. Then the rope tightened mercilessly while Buck struggled in fury, **his tongue lolling out of his mouth** and **his great chest panting**.

2. She was now standing arms akimbo, **her shoulders drooping a little, her head cocked to one side, her glasses winking in the sunlight**.

3. It ran, **its pelvic bones crushing aside trees and bushes, its taloned feet clawing damp earth**, leaving prints six inches deep wherever it settled its weight.

4. And then, **his feet sinking in the soft nap of the carpet, his hand in one pocket clutching the money**, he felt as if he could squeal or laugh out loud.

5. Within, you could hear the sighs and murmurs as the furthest chambers of it died, **the organs malfunctioning, liquids running a final instant from pocket to sac to spleen, everything shutting off**, closing up forever.

Practice 4 (page 57)

1. One customer in the line spoke out and ranted continuously about the unfair price, the other customers rallying and demanding the same reduction in the cost.

2. Several dancers near the band joined together and moved quickly into two lines, one couple heading and leading the rest through the complicated steps.

Practice 5 (pages 57–59)

1. The youngest brother was nearby resting, **all his work over**.

2. As soon as it was over, they pranced around Gracie like courtiers, **Paul wooing her disgustingly with his stretched smiles**.

3. Later, very happy, he held the baby soothingly, and brought the music box to her and wound the toy up, **his voice singing with it**.

4. The student teacher erased everything quickly and, with a hurried cover-up, started to call out the spelling words for us, **her embarrassment coming from her misspelling on the chalkboard**.

Practice 7 (pages 61–62)

1. The town lay on a broad estuary, **its old yellow plastered buildings hugging the beach**.

2. Like giants they toiled, **days flashing on the heels of days like dreams as they heaped the treasure up**.

3. An Arab on a motorcycle, **his long robes flying in the wind of his speed**, passed John at such a clip that the spirals of dust from his turnings on the winding road looked like little tornadoes.

4. In solid phalanxes the leaders crowded about the three jaguars, **tusks thrust forward, their little eyes bloodshot with anger and with battle lust**.

Practice 8 (pages 62–63)

1. I could hear him crashing down the hill toward the sea, **the frightening laughter echoing back**.

2. Finny and I went along the Boardwalk in our sneakers and white slacks, **Finny in a light blue polo shirt and I in a T-shirt**.

3. All the time he was reading the newspaper, his wife, a fat woman with a white face, leaned out of the window, gazing into the street, **her thick white arms folded under her loose breast on the window sill**.

4. To the right of them the gym meditated behind its gray walls, **the high, wide, oval-topped windows shining back at the sun**.

Practice 9 (pages 63–64)

1. Now, in the waning daylight, he turned into Glover Street toward his home, **his arms swinging as he moved onto the unpaved road**.

2. As they drove off Wilson saw her standing under the big tree, looking pretty rather than beautiful in her faintly rosy khaki, **her dark hair drawn back off her forehead and gathered in a knot low on her neck, her face as fresh, he thought, as though she were in England**.

3. His great chest was low to the ground, **his head forward and down, his feet flying like mad, the claws scarring the hard-packed snow in parallel grooves**.

4. In front of the house where we lived, the mountain went down steeply to the little plain along the lake, and we sat on the porch of the house in the sun and saw the winding of the road down the mountain-side and the terraced vineyards on the side of the lower mountain, **the vines all dead now for the**

winter and **the fields divided by stone walls**, and below
the vineyards, **the houses of the town on the narrow plain
along the lake shore**.

Practice 10 (page 64)

1. He began scrambling up the wooden pegs nailed to the side of
   the tree, **his back muscles working like a panther's**.

2. Touser roused himself under Fowler's desk and scratched
   another flea, **his leg thumping hard against the floor**.

3. They were smiling, **one woman talking, the others
   listening**.

4. Wearing an Indian dhoti, **his forehead annointed with a
   red dot**, bald, slight, with a bony face, deep-set eyes the size
   of peas, **his body skeletal, his feet in velvet slippers**, he
   sat on a hard wooden chair, at center stage, tucking his legs
   under him in a yogic manner.

   Oscar Hijuelos, Mr. Ives' Christmas

Focus 7
Appositive Phrase

Practice 1 (pages 67–68)
The appositive phrase is in **boldface**. <u>Underlining</u> indicates the
word that the appositive phrase identifies.

1. The <u>writer</u>, **an old man with a white mustache**, had some
   difficulty in getting into bed. (subject-verb split)

2. Halfway there he heard the <u>sound</u> he dreaded, **the hollow,
   rasping cough of a horse**. (sentence closer)

3. <u>Mr. Mick Malloy</u>, **cashier at the Ulster and Connaught
   Bank**, draped his grey sports jacket neatly on a hanger and
   put on his black shantung work coat. (subject-verb split)

4. **A self-educated man**, <u>he</u> had accepted the necessary
   smattering of facts of science with a serene indulgence, as
   simply so much further proof of what the Creator could do
   when He put His hand to it. (sentence opener)

Practice 2 (pages 68–69)

1. She struggled as usual to maintain her calm, composed, friendly bearing, **a sort of mask she wore all over her body**.

2. The judge, **an old, bowlegged fellow in a pale-blue sweater**, had stopped examining the animals and was reading over some notes he had taken on the back of a dirty envelope.

3. A man, **a weary old pensioner with a bald dirty head and a stained brown corduroy waistcoat**, appeared at the door of a small gate lodge.

Practice 3 (pages 69–70)

1. One of them, **a slender young man with white hands, the son of a jeweler in Winesburg**, talked continually of virginity.

2. In the late afternoon Will Henderson, **owner and editor of the *Eagle***, went over to Tom Willy's saloon.

3. The sound of the approaching grain teams was louder, **thud of big hooves on hard ground, drag of brakes**, and **the jingle of trace chains**.

4. Once Enoch Bentley, **the older one of the boys**, struck his father, **old Tom Bentley**, with the butt of a teamster's whip, and the old man seemed likely to die.

5. Mr. Mick Malloy, **tall, young secret gambler with devil-may-care eyes and a long humorous nose**, became Mr. Malloy, **tall cashier with a dignified face, a gentlemanly bank clerk, a nice sort of fellow**.

Practice 4 (pages 70–71)

1. By the podium scholarly Henrietta stood, intelligent and composed and smiling, **president and valedictorian of the senior class**.

2. Under the canopy they danced, beaming and affectionate and happy, **bride and groom in their finery**.

Practice 5 (pages 71–74)

1. Near the statue was an obvious tourist, **an older lady with a Kodak camera**.

2. *Gone with the Wind*, **the movie with the most re-issues**, originated as a novel of the old South by an unglamorous and unknown authoress.

3. "Missouri" is a special casserole, **a blend of potatoes and stewed tomatoes and hamburger**.

4. We were far from our destination and were making good time on the interstate, but no time to squander, and Dad wouldn't stop more than twice a day although we kids were itchy, and Mom, who kept the peace, **a shrewd, gentle arbitrator with Solomon's mind**, circumvented some flare-ups, and those she couldn't she left to Heaven.

Practice 7 (pages 75–76)

1. On this Sunday morning the postman and the policeman had gone fishing in the boat of Mr. Corell, **the popular storekeeper**.

2. The real estate agent, **an old man with a smiling, hypocritical face**, soon joined them.

3. They approached the domed synagogue with its iron weathercock, **a pock-marked yellow-walled building with an oak door**, for the time being resting in peace.

4. Lieutenant Tonder was a poet, **a bitter poet who dreamed of perfect, ideal love of elevated young men for poor girls**.

Practice 8 (pages 76–77)

1. At the gate, I show the pass to a young Japanese private, **the sentry**.

2. When he was twelve, his mother married an executive of a machine tool company in Cleveland, **an engineer who had adult children of his own**.

3. **A modern intelligent woman**, my patient with her five children seemed in many ways as trapped as her forebears in Victorian times before the emancipation of women.

4. On the bark of the tree was scored the name of Deacon Peabody, **an eminent man**, who had waxed wealthy by driving shrewd bargains with the Indians.

Practice 9 (page 78)

1. Thus, one noontime, coming back from the office lunch downstairs a little earlier than usual, he found her and several of the foreign-family girls, as well as four of the American girls, surrounding Polish Mary, **one of the gayest and roughest of the foreign-family girls**, who was explaining in rather a high key how a certain "feller" whom she had met the night before had given her a beaded bag, and for what purpose.

2. The rest were standing around in hatless, smoky little groups of twos and threes and fours inside the heated waiting room, talking in voices that, almost without exception, sounded collegiately dogmatic, as though each young man, in his strident, conversational turn, was clearing up, once and for all, some highly controversial issue, **one that the outside, non-matriculating world had been bungling, provocatively or not, for centuries**.

3. Out in the distance the fans of windmills twinkled, turning, and about the base of each, about the drink tank, was a speckle of dark dots, **a herd of cattle grazing in moonlight and meditating upon good grass, block salt, impermanence, and love**.

4. Perhaps two or three times a year we would come together at a party, one of those teen-age affairs which last until dawn with singing and dancing and silly games such as "Kiss the Pillow," or "Post Office," **the game which permits one to call for the creature of one's choice and embrace her furtively in a dark room**.

Practice 10 (pages 78–79)

1. My bed was an army cot, **one of those affairs which are made wide enough to sleep on comfortably only by putting up, flat with the middle section, the two sides which ordinarily hang down like the sideboards of a drop-leaf table**.

2. He, **the enlightened man who looks afar in the dark**, had fled because of his superior perceptions and knowledge.

3. I had hardly any patience with the serious work of life which, now that it stood between me and desire, seemed to me child's play, **ugly monotonous child's play**.

4. There was Major Hunter, **a haunted little man of figures, a little man who, being a dependable unit, considered all other men either as dependable units or as unfit to live**.

Focus 8
Participial Phrase

Practice 1 (pages 83–84)

The participial phrase is in **boldface**. Underlining indicates the word that the participial phrase modifies.

1. <u>Manuel</u>, **lying on the ground**, kicked at the bull's muzzle with his slippered feet. (subject-verb split)

2. **Clutching the clawing kitten to her collarbone**, her hair in her open mouth, <u>she</u> bawled encouragement to them. (sentence opener)

3. <u>They</u> were diggers in clay, **transformed by lantern light into a race of giants**. (sentence closer)

4. <u>Ruthie</u>, **dressed in a real dress of pink muslin that came below her knees**, was a little serious in her young-ladyness. (subject-verb split)

Practice 2 (pages 84–85)

1. Bernard, **wearing a black turtleneck sweater, dirty flannels, and slippers**, was waiting on the landing outside.

2. **Sitting up in bed eating breakfast**, we could see the lake and the mountains across the lake on the French side.

3. **Coming down the pole**, I had a sense of being whirled violently through the air, with no control over my movements.

4. A little house, **perched on high piles**, appeared black in the distance.

5. When we had made our way downstairs, we saw the woman with the lovely complexion, Miss Pilzer, **screaming** and **begging to be allowed to go with her mother**.

Practice 3 (pages 85–86)

1. He was a blind beggar, **carrying the traditional battered cane** and **thumping his way before him with the cautious, half-furtive effort of the sightless**.

2. The passengers, **emerging from the mildewed dimness of the customs shed, blinking their eyes against the blinding sunlight**, all had the look of invalids crawling into the hospital on their last legs.

3. That winter my mother and brother came, and we set up housekeeping, **buying furniture on the installment plan, being cheated, and yet knowing no way to avoid it**.

4. **Jumping to his feet** and **breaking off the tale**, Doctor Parcival began to walk up and down in the office of the *Winesburg Eagle*, where George Willard sat listening.

5. A young Mexican woman, **softened and dispirited by recent childbirth, dressed in the elegant, perpetual mourning of her caste**, came up slowly, **leaning on the arm of the Indian nurse who carried her baby**, his long embroidered robe streaming over her arm almost to the ground.

Practice 4 (page 87)

1. As her arm whirled fast over the egg-whites, her face shifted toward the cookbook and stared at it, grimacing and expressing confusion and frustration over the third direction in the recipe that listed and explained more and ever more of the procedure.

2. After Jo-Jo climbed higher onto the counter, he pulled on the doors and looked for the candy, stretching but missing jars and boxes in the rear with bright colors that beckoned but hid farther and farther from his reach.

Practice 5 (pages 88–90)

1. A pile of new debris cluttered up the driveway, and the tenants, **gazing at the disgrace**, watched with heavy hearts.

2. The dog sat up, his mouth clenching the rolled newspaper, **wagging his tail**, and begged a reward.

3. The upholstered pieces, the expensive, polished tables had been moved into the huge dining room, **covered with endless painter's cloths so that they would be protected from the splatterings of paint**.

4. The meeting that had been like a marathon among meetings continued, and the leader deliberated about his strategy, **stalling after the last remarks from the representative with whom he had planned so many emergency ploys focusing upon every conceivable tactic for the suppression of the opposition**.

Practice 7 (pages 92–94)

1. **Lying on the floor of the flat-car with the guns beside me under the canvas**, I was wet, cold, and very hungry.

2. There was a tattered man, **fouled with dust, blood, and powder stain from hair to shoes**, who trudged quietly at the youth's side.

3. I brought the boat up to the stone pier, and the barman pulled in the line, **coiling it on the bottom of the boat** and **hooking the spinner on the edge of the gunwale**.

4. The trail moved up the dry shale hillside, **avoiding rocks, dropping under clefts, climbing in and out of old water scars**.

Practice 8 (pages 94–95)

1. **Bleeding profusely and cut off from his supply of eagles' blood**, he had never been closer to death.

2. In an upstairs bedroom, shortly before dawn, a young American mother sat on the edge of a steel-framed bed, **rocking her nursing daughter**.

3. By and by, one group after another came struggling back to the mouth of the cave, **panting**, hilarious, **smeared from head to foot with tallow drippings, daubed with clay**, and **entirely delighted with the success of the day**.

4. Adolph Knipe took a sip of stout, **tasting the malty-bitter flavor, feeling the trickle of cold liquid as it traveled down his throat and settled in the top of his stomach**,

cool at first, **then spreading and becoming warm, making a little area of warmness inside him**.

Practice 9 (pages 95–96)
1. With the core of the reel showing, his heart feeling stopped with excitement, **leaning back against the current that mounted icily up his thighs**, Nick thumbed the reel hard with his left hand.

2. Mrs. Carpenter was putting sun-tan oil on Sybil's shoulders, **spreading it down over the delicate, wing-like blades of her back**.

3. Soon the men began to gather, **surveying their own children, speaking of planting and rain, tractors and taxes**.

4. The *Carpathia* ship's passengers pitched in gallantly to help the survivors of the *Titanic*, **providing extra toothbrushes, lending clothes, sewing smocks for the children out of steamer blankets brought along in the lifeboats**.

Practice 10 (page 96)
1. The children crawled over the shelves and into the potato and onion bins, **twanging all the time in their sharp voices like cigar-box guitars**.

2. And he, **sensing a new and strange and quite terrified note in all this the moment he read it**, at once looked over his shoulder at her and, **seeing her face so white and drawn**, signaled that he would meet her.

3. In the late afternoon, the truck came back, **bumping and rattling through the dust**, and there was a layer of dust in the bed, and the hood was covered with dust, and the headlights were obscured with a red flour.

4. He stood there, **balancing on one leg** and **holding tightly to the edges of the window sill with his hands, staring at the sign and at the whitewashed lettering of the words**.

Focus 9
Reviewing the Structures

Practice 1 (pages 97–98)

1. Participial

2. Appositive

3. Participial (past)

4. Absolutes

5. Absolutes

6. Absolute

7. Participial

8. Participial (past)

9. Appositive

10. Appositives

11. Participial

12. Appositives

Practice 4 (pages 102–103)

1. One participial, one absolute

2. One absolute, one participial

3. Two absolutes, one participial

4. One appositive, one absolute

5. One appositive, one absolute

6. Two absolutes, one participial

7. One absolute, one participial

8. Two participials, one past and the other present

9. One participial, two absolutes

10. Three participials, one present and the others past

11. Three participials, one appositive

12. One participial, one absolute

Focus 10
Sentence Openers

Practice 1 (pages 107–109)

1. **In the biggest press conference that I had ever experienced anywhere**, the camera bulbs flashed, and the reporters fired questions.

2. **Without a word**, she took a piece of paper out of her pants pocket.

3. **Even then, when we might have kissed and embraced unrestrainedly**, our shyness prevented us from sharing anything but the most innocent pleasure.

4. **Before the girls got to the porch**, I heard their laughter crackling and popping like pine logs in a cooking stove.

5. **Through the burial in Pleasant Memory Cemetery and the car trip home, through the flurry of reclaiming the children, setting up the coffeepot, and greeting the guests who stopped by afterward**, Ian wandered in a dreamlike state of mind.

6. **Being a star in her own right, earning twenty-five pounds a week**, she was well able to support herself and her children.

7. **Now, facing the bull**, he was conscious of many things at the same time.

8. **There, between two trees, against a background of gaunt black rocks**, was a figure from a dream, a strange beast that was horned and drunken-legged, but like something he had never even imagined.

Practice 2 (pages 109–110)
1. **At last, after what seemed hours**, my turn came.

2. **Behind and in front of us**, other children trotted in twos and
   threes.

3. **On the very next try a few days later**, everything was
   perfect, even the punctuation.

4. **In the end, after several months of work**, he had
   persuaded something like seventy percent of the writers on his
   list to sign the contract.

5. **Upon the half decayed veranda of a small frame house
   that stood near the edge of a ravine near the town of
   Winesburg, Ohio**, a fat little old man walked nervously up
   and down.

6. **Suffering, sick, and angry, but also grimly satisfied with
   his new stoicism**, he stood there leaning on his rifle, and
   watched the seething black mound grow smaller.

Practice 3 (pages 110–111)
1. At the dumpster, when the truck arrived with junk, they
   emptied it out in minutes piling up the garbage, and as they
   pulled away and started the turn near Canal Street much too
   fast, the remaining debris began to clank in the back and near
   the cabin and to shift with thuds.

2. From the start, because the store had opened with haste,
   Jackson pondered constantly in dread during the day
   wondering about his boss, and because he had been up late
   last night and had the alarm in the morning set too late, he
   dragged himself at eight o'clock to open up the store and the
   prepayment office and to worry over his possible
   punishment.

Practice 4 (pages 111–113)
1. **After meeting with the President**, he signed and delivered
   the letter to the secretary.

2. **After she tried the choreography**, she met the director, and
   they planned to confer with the producer.

3. **Through all the ups and downs of the trial**, the lawyers and the judge, the defendant and the jury, had been intense listeners to the expert testimony.

4. **Too pleasant to fight with the customer about the return, and too agreeable to resist**, Miss Simpson agreed with a smile, refunded the money without protest, and remained remarkably calm.

Practice 6 (pages 114–116)

1. **Within a week**, the manuscript had been read and accepted by an enthusiastic publisher.

2. **Like silent, hungry sharks that swim in the darkness of the sea**, the German submarines arrived in the middle of the night.

3. **Sitting beside his flowering window while the panes rattled and the wind blew in under the door**, Rosicky gave himself to reflection as he had not done since those Sundays in the loft of the furniture factory in New York, long ago.

4. **Crouched on the edge of the plateau**, the schoolmaster looked at the deserted expanse.

5. **And then, his feet sinking in the soft nap of the carpet, his hand in one pocket clutching the money**, he felt as if he could squeal or laugh out loud.

6. **Soiled by the filth of a strange city, spat upon by unknown mouths, driven from the streets into the roadway, carrying the heaviest loads upon his back, scurrying between carriages, carts, and horses, staring death in the eyes every moment**, he still kept silent.

Practice 7 (pages 116–118)

1. **Remaining single**, a man converts himself into a permanent public temptation.

2. **Pain shooting up my entire arm**, I lay panting on the edge of the pool and gingerly began to feel my wrist.

3. **Pretending to take an interest in the New Season's Models**, Gumbril made, squinting sideways over the burning tip of his cigar, an inventory of her features.

4. **In the frosty December dusk**, their cabins looked neat and snug with pale blue smoke rising from the chimneys and doorways glowing amber from the fires inside.

5. **In the darkness in the hallway by the door**, the sick woman arose and started again toward her own room.

6. **In her girlhood and before her marriage with Tom Willard**, Elizabeth had borne a somewhat shaky reputation in Winesburg.

7. **Near the edge of town**, the group had to walk around an automobile burned and squatting on the narrow road, and the bearers on one side, unable to see their way in the darkness, fell into a deep ditch.

8. **By nightfall of an average courting day**, a fiddler crab who has been standing on tiptoe for eight or ten hours waving a heavy claw in the air is in pretty sad shape.

Practice 8 (pages 118–119)

1. **Next day**, we rode to the hospital in a carriage with a horse.

2. **As she grew older and handsomer**, she had many beaux, but these small-town boys didn't interest her.

3. **In her own mind**, the tall dark girl had been in those days much confused.

4. **When the night crept down in shadowy blue and silver**, they threaded the shimmering channel in the rowboat and, tying it to a jutting rock, began climbing the cliff together.

5. **In the late afternoon**, the truck came back, bumping and rattling through the dust, and there was a layer of dust in the bed, and the hood was covered with dust, and the headlights were obscured with a red flour.

6. **To a man so newly lonely, so newly alone**, an invitation out meant an evening in other people's lives, and therefore freedom from his own, and it meant the possibility of laughter that would surprise him—how good it was to be alive and healthy, to have a body that had not given up in spite of everything.

7. **Whenever she lay awake beside her husband, like tonight**, she would still keep her eyes closed for a long time, then open them and relish with astonishment the blue of the

brand-new curtains, replacing the apricot-pink which had filtered with the morning light into the room where she had slept as a girl.

8. **Tugged here and there in his stockinged feet, bewildered by the numbers, staggered by so much raw flesh**, Dr. Sasaki lost all sense of profession and stopped working as a skillful surgeon and a sympathetic man; he became an automaton, mechanically wiping, daubing, winding, wiping, daubing, winding.

Focus 11
Subject-Verb Splits

Practice 1 (pages 122–123)

1. The writer, **an old man with a white mustache**, had some difficulty in getting into bed.

2. When Jesse Bentley, **absorbed in his own idea**, suddenly arose and advanced toward him, his terror grew until his whole body shook.

3. The twins, **smeary in the face, eating steadily from untidy paper sacks of sweets**, followed them in a detached way.

4. His hands, **beyond control**, ran up and down the soft-skinned baby body, the sinuous, limbless body.

5. One of them, **a slender young man with white hands, the son of a jeweler in Winesburg**, talked continually of virginity.

6. His face, **fresh from the pounding of Johnnie's fists**, felt more pleasure than pain in the wind and the driving snow.

7. The big hands, **with the knotted, cracked joints and the square, horn-thick nails**, hang loose off the wrist bone like clumsy, homemade tools hung on the wall.

8. The four pretty, slatternly Spanish girls, **their dark hair sleeked down over their ears, their thin-soled black slippers too short in the toes and badly run over at high heels**, took leisurely leave, with kisses all around, of a half dozen local young men, who had brought flowers and baskets of fruit.

Practice 2 (page 124)

1. In the flurry of traffic, the ambulance driver, **who only an hour ago had been asleep**, gripped the steering wheel, and his siren, **wailing like a giant in agony**, warned the traffic to make way.

2. Near the field of wheat, tough-skinned Jasper, **who a year ago had been an irresponsible drunk**, walked peacefully among his crops, and his serenity, **derived from his year's self-control with alcohol**, allowed him to concentrate on farming.

Practice 3 (pages 126–127)

1. Nielsen Rating Service, **a determiner of TV ratings that had been accepted by the TV networks that season**, was surveying this morning.

2. The cook, **a fine-bellied gourmet**, was back in the kitchen at the closet freezer, ruminating about the latest beef selections, and the butcher reassured him.

3. Because the thunderstorm, **which was sudden and fierce in downpour**, brought to fields the rain for the crops and was steady enough to remain in the parched land and penetrate to the roots, the plants raised their branches and arched their stems toward the sun.

4. Janice Larson, **who successfully finished auto-mechanics, having been one of few girls in the course**, tried with great persistence for a related job and applied to several employment agencies, where counselors were surprised at her sex, describing her prospects with guarded optimism and sincere hope.

Practice 5 (pages 128–129)

1. The other sniper, **seeing the cap and rifle fall**, thought that he had killed his man.

2. Manuel, **standing in the hallway**, felt there was someone in the room.

3. The bull, **in full gallop**, pivoted and charged the cape, his head down, his tail rising.

4. The members of the cuadrilla, **who had been watching the burlesque from the runway between the barrera and the**

seats, came walking back and stood in a group talking, under the electric light in the patio.

5. He found that the older ones, **those who were running out of ideas and had taken to drink**, were the easiest to handle.

6. A succession of loud and shrill screams, **bursting suddenly from the throat of the chained form**, seemed to thrust me violently back.

Practice 6 (pages 129–130)

1. When the match went out, the old man, **trembling from agitation**, peeped into the little window.

2. The country house, **on this particular wintry afternoon**, was most enjoyable.

3. At once Buntaro slid an arrow from the quiver and, **still sitting**, set up the bow, raised it, drew back the bowstring to eye level and released the shaft with savage, almost poetic liquidity.

4. These three trains, **motionless in the moonlight**, confirmed my fears that traffic was not maintained by night on this part of the line.

5. The first opportune minute came that very afternoon, and Cress, **after being warned**, went in tears to her room.

6. And my departure, which, **especially in my own eyes**, stank of betrayal, was my only means of proving, or redeeming, that love, my only hope.

7. Only a frying pan, **with an arrow through it**, remained.

8. His little dark eyes, **deepset under a tanned forehead**, and his mouth, **surrounded with wrinkles**, made him look attentive and studious.

Practice 7 (pages 131–132)

1. During the first year of imprisonment, the lawyer, **as far as it was possible to judge from his short notes**, suffered terribly from loneliness and boredom.

2. While we were waiting for the coffee, the headwaiter, **with an ingratiating smile on his false face**, came up to us bearing a large basket full of huge peaches.

3. Doubletree Mutt came sideways and embarrassed up through the vegetable patch, and Jody, **remembering how he had thrown the clod**, put his arm about the dog's neck and kissed him on his wide black nose.

4. Her gaze, **deceiving, transforming her to her imaginings**, changed the contour of her sallow-skinned face, skillfully refashioning her long-pointed nose on which a small chilly tear had gathered.

5. She, **thrilled and in part seduced by his words, instead of resisting as definitely as she would have in any other case**, now gazed at him, fascinated by his enthusiasm.

6. The mouth-organist, **now revealed as a motherly middle-aged woman with a large and rather dignified wart on her nose**, got up and began dancing up and down the aisle, playing the instrument with one hand and flouncing up her skirts with the other as she jiggled in time to an old music-hall number. . . .

7. Nick's heart, **under the bone and muscle of his great chest**, swelled with sweet thoughts of his wife and child, who lived in a foreign city across an ocean.

8. And he, **sensing a new and strange and quite terrified note in all this the moment he read it**, at once looked over his shoulder at her and, **seeing her face so white and drawn**, signaled that he would meet her.

Practice 8 (pages 132–133)

1. The Irish, **like all the Celts**, stripped before battle and rushed their enemy naked, carrying sword and shield but wearing only sandals. . . .

2. Once Enoch Bentley, **the older one of the boys**, struck his father, old Tom Bentley, with the butt of a teamster's whip, and the old man seemed likely to die.

3. McCaslin, **still propped on his elbow**, watched until the other's shadow sank down the wall and vanished, becoming one with the mass of sleeping shadows.

4. The big hands, **with the knotted, cracked joints and the square, horn-thick nails**, hang loose off the wrist bone like clumsy, homemade tools hung on the wall of a shed.

5. And Clyde, **realizing that for some reason he must not say more**, had not the courage or persistence or the background to go further with her now, went for his coat, and, **looking sadly but obediently back at her**, departed.

Focus 12
Sentence Closers

Practice 1 (pages 135–137)

1. He went on, **limping**.

2. She was separated from Grandpa, **for what reason neither grand-parent would tell**.

3. It was a heavy sound, **hard and sharp, not rolling**.

4. And so we went to the station, across the meadow, **taking the longer way, trying to be together as long as possible**.

5. Sometimes a gaggle of them came to the store, **filling the whole room, chasing out the air and even changing the well-known scents**.

6. Hour after hour he stood there silent, **motionless, a shadow carved in ebony and moonlight**.

7. Prometheus was one of the Titans, **a gigantic race who inhabited the earth before the creation of man**.

8. Light flickered on bits of ruby glass and on sensitive capillary hairs in the nylon-brushed nostrils of the creature that quivered gently, gently, **its eight legs spidered under it on rubber-padded paws**.

Practice 2 (pages 137–138)

1. Buck stood and looked on, **the successful champion, the dominant primordial beast who had made his kill and found it good**.

2. The Arab was asleep, **hunched up near the blankets now, his mouth open, utterly relaxed**.

3. That winter my mother and brother came, and we set up housekeeping, **buying furniture on the installment plan, being cheated and yet knowing no way to avoid it.**

4. Six boys came over the hill, **half an hour early that afternoon, running hard, their heads down, their forearms working, their breath whistling.**

5. She was always up there somewhere, **high above me, like some goddess whom I had discovered and regarded as my very own.**

6. Father lay crumpled up on the stone floor of the pantry, **face down, arms twisted at a curious angle, clad just in his vest and trousers, feet bare.**

Practice 3 (page 138)

1. They would meet, **deciding about their agenda for the sales meeting, their opinions uncertain, their interest high, the leader of the group of section chiefs shouting out like a huckster.**

2. She smiled, **glancing at the flowers in the vase, their stems poised, their blossoms in full bloom, the arrangement of the bouquet of roses looking like a prizewinner.**

Practice 4 (pages 139–141)

1. High up the tree there climbed some girls, **little adventurers who imagined a great escapade of nearly Everest proportions.**

2. Inspecting the plumbing and fixtures that outfitted the new bathroom, he walked around, **his tappings and probings done with his expert skill, and his experience guiding his assessment of the work.**

3. They could foresee a time of soldiers ending their battles, and a period of permanent truce, **negotiating their disputes about politics, and many of the old arguments, living peacefully within dissent.**

4. Then it was graduation, and they were encouraged by a dream of new beginnings for their lives, **marching among friends and proud parents, dressed in their caps and gowns as the orchestra, with lusty fanfares, stirred them with its**

majesty of the pomp of trumpet blares and the circumstances of the formal rite of passage.

Practice 6 (pages 142–144)
1. I seemed forever condemned, **ringed by walls**.

2. I waited for Andries at the back of the queue, **out of the reach of the white man's mocking eyes**.

3. The Fog Horn was blowing steadily, **once every fifteen seconds**.

4. Gradually his head began to revolve, **slowly, rhythmically**.

5. Down on the little landing-bay were three cottages in a row, **like coast guards' cottages, all neat and whitewashed**.

6. He spent long, silent hours in his study, **working not very fast, nor very importantly, letting the writing spin softly from him as if it were drowsy gossamer**.

Practice 7 (pages 144–146)
1. The little boy stared at Ferris, **amazed and unbelieving**.

2. I came out crawling, **clinging to the handle of the door until I made sure of my bearings**.

3. Nick fought him against the current, **letting him thump in the water against the spring of the rod**.

4. Hattie sat down at her old Spanish table, **watching them in the cloudly warmth of the day, clasping her hands, chuckling and sad**.

5. Nick climbed out onto the meadow and stood, **water running down his trousers and out of his shoes, his shoes squlchy**.

6. He walked with a prim strut, **swinging out his legs in a half-circle with each step, his heels biting smartly into the red velvet carpet on the floor**.

7. The old woman slid to the edge of her chair and leaned forward, **shading her eyes from the piercing sunset with her hand**.

8. The horse galloped along wearily under the murky morning sky, **dragging his old rattling box after his heels**, and Gabriel was again in a cab with her, **galloping to catch the boat, galloping to their honeymoon**.

Practice 8 (pages 146–147)

1. She stood out from all the other girls in the school, **like someone with blue blood in her veins**.

2. His face was fleshy and pallid, **touched with colour only at the thick hanging lobes of his ears and at the wide wings of his nose**.

3. Todd's hands were clenched into fists, **hiding the butchered nails**.

4. His earnestness affected the boy, **who presently became silent and a little alarmed**.

5. Ian appeared at the back door, **lugging a large cardboard box**.

6. Mary Jane gazed after her, **a moody puzzled expression on her face, while Mrs. Conroy leaned over the banisters to listen for the hall-door**.

7. As far down the long stretch as he could see, the trout were rising, **making circles all down the surface of the water, as though it were starting to rain**.

8. The girl at first did not return any of the kisses, but presently she began to, and after she had put several on his cheek, she reached his lips and remained there, **kissing him again and again as if she were trying to draw all the breath out of him**.

Focus 13
Reviewing the Positions

Practice 1 (pages 148–155)

1. Positions: **opener, closer**

    a. *Around the old gravestones*, <u>the grass was high</u>,

    b. *untended*.

2. Positions: **opener, closer**

   a. *As they swung on the turn*, <u>the sled went over</u>,

   b. *spilling half its load through the loose lashings.*

3. Positions: **opener, closer**

   a. *When she awoke several hours later*, <u>Snow White saw the faces of seven bearded, vertically challenged men</u>,

   b. *surrounding the bed.*

4. Positions: **subject-verb split, closer**

   Fletcher Seagull,

   a. *who loved aerobatics like no one else*, <u>conquered his sixteen-point vertical slow roll and the next day topped it off with a triple cartwheel</u>,

   b. *his feathers flashing white sunlight to a beach from which more than one furtive eye watched.*

5. Positions: **opener, closer**

   a. *Subdued*, <u>I fixed my attention upon Reverend Sykes</u>,

   b. *who seemed to be waiting for me to settle down.*

6. Positions: **opener, closer**

   a. *Wildly*, <u>Alfred bolted across the street</u>,

   b. *sidestepping a taxicab by inches*

   c. *ignoring the horns and curses of braking drivers.*

7. Positions: **opener, closer**

   a. *In the far corner*, <u>the man was still asleep</u>,

   b. *snoring slightly on the intaking breath,*

   c. *his head back against the wall.*

8. Positions: **opener, closer**

   a. *At night*, <u>she looked at the bright stars</u>,

   b. *sleeping little,*

   c. *listening to the river.*

9. Positions: **subject-verb split, closer**

   <u>A big kitchen table</u>,

a. *covered with one of those old-fashioned oilcloths*, was neatly set as if for a big party,

b. *with eight chairs,*

c. *two on each side of the table.*

10. Positions: **opener, closer**

a. *An excellent student*, <u>Caroline received uniformly high grades</u>,

b. *which she worked hard to get,*

c. *doing more than two hours of homework each day.*

11. Positions: **opener, closer**

a. *At the cemetery*, <u>my brothers and I buried mother</u>,

b. *taking our time speaking to her,*

c. *as though she could hear us.*

12. Positions: **opener, closer**

a. *His face lit by flames*, <u>across the open hearth sat my father</u>,

b. *leaning forward,*

c. *his hands outspread to his knees,*

d. *his shoulders tense.*

13. Positions: **opener, closer**

a. *Beyond the driver,*

b. *beyond the windshield*, <u>a structure appeared</u>,

c. *indistinct,*

d. *unidentifiable.*

14. Positions: **opener, closer**

a. *Across the tops*

b. *of about a hundred gravestones and many people*, <u>I saw Viola in her black dress</u>,

c. *standing on a little rise,*

d. *her gray hair wandering from its knot.*

15. Positions: **opener, closer**

    a. *In an upstairs bedroom,*

    b. *shortly*

    c. *before dawn*, a young American mother sat on the edge of a steel-framed bed,

    d. *rocking her nursing daughter.*

16. Positions: **opener, closer**

    a. *Periodically*, wheelchair vans or ambulances or private cars parked in front of the portico, and new residents were escorted in,

    b. *a few on their own feet,*

    c. *others in wheelchairs,*

    d. *some on gurneys.*

17. Positions: **opener, closer**

    a. *Outside the window*, Roland has stopped chopping and is sitting on the chopping block,

    b. *his arms on his knees,*

    c. *his big hands dangling,*

    d. *staring off into the trees.*

18. Positions: **opener, closer**

    a. *On the last, cold day*

    b. *of December*

    c. *in the year 406*, the river Rhine froze solid,

    d. *providing the natural bridge the hundreds of thousands of hungry men, women, and children had been waiting for.*

19. Positions: **opener, closer**

    a. *At the university,*

    b. *in his gray suit*, he had seemed of no more than medium height,

    c. *perhaps because he stooped so attentively to hear the slightest word from the person he was talking to,*

    d. *perhaps because his neat, fair hair made him look somehow ineffectual.*

20. Positions: **opener, closer**

    a. *At three forty-five,* <u>he came up to the house again and said good-bye to the children,</u>

    b. *who were seated on the porch,*

    c. *drinking apple juice* and

    d. *eating graham crackers* and

    e. *rolling pebbles back and forth.*

21. Positions: **opener, subject-verb split**

    a. *After rain,* or

    b. *when snowfalls thaw,* <u>the streets,</u>

    c. *unnamed,*

    d. *unshaded,*

    e. *unpaved,* <u>turn from the thickest dust into the direst mud.</u>

22. Positions: **opener, closer**

    a. *Shifting the weight of the line to his shoulder* and

    b. *kneeling carefully,* <u>he washed his hand in the ocean and held it there for more than a minute,</u>

    c. *submerged,*

    d. *watching the blood trail away and the steady movement of the water against his hand*

    e. *as the boat moved.*

23. Positions: **opener, closer**

    a. *On occasions,*

    b. *when the tide ran exceptionally high,* <u>waves washed perilously close to the lighthouse,</u>

    c. *dashing its base*

    d. *with salt-tinged algae,*

    e. *which clung to it now like a sea moss.*

24. Positions: **opener, closer**

    a. *Turning,*

    b. *his shoulder pressing against the wall,* <u>he moved</u>

    c. *until he was standing sideways,*

    d. *his feet together on the narrow ledge,*

    e. *his side hugging the wall,*

    f. *as he faced the wide opening.*

25. Positions: **opener, closer**

    a. *Blindly,* <u>his right hand flew over the ledge,</u>

    b. *his fingers dancing across it,*

    c. *reaching,*

    d. *feeling,*

    e. *searching*

    f. *until his body began to drop.*

26. Positions: **opener, subject-verb split**

    a. *In the morning,*

    b. *breakfastless* and

    c. *shaky*

    d. *from seven cups*

    e. *of coffee,* <u>Quoyle,</u>

    f. *heart and stomach aching,* <u>went to the wharf on his way to Wavey</u>.

27. Positions: **opener, closer**

    a. *Through the thicket,*

    b. *across the river,* and

c. *in the deep, deep woods,* <u>lived a family of bears</u>,

d. *a Papa bear,*

e. *a Mama Bear,* and

f. *a Baby Bear,*

g. *who all lived together anthropomorphically in a little cottage as a nuclear family.*

28. Positions: **opener, closer**

a. *When Laurel was a child,* <u>she was sent to sleep</u>

b. *by the beloved reading voice*

c. *under a velvety cloak*

d. *of words,*

d. *patterned richly* and

e. *stitched with gold,*

f. *coming straight out*

g. *of a fairy tale,*

h. *while the voice went on reading aloud into her dreams.*

29. Positions: **subject-verb split, closer**

<u>The sun</u>,

a. *red* and

b. *enormous,* <u>began to sink</u>

c. *into the western sky,*

d. *the moon beginning to rise*

e. *on the other side*

f. *of the river*

g. *with its own glorious shade*

h. *of red,*

i. *coming up out of the trees like a russet firebird.*

30. Positions: **opener, closer**

   a. *In the half-light,* <u>*my eyes roamed*</u>

   b. *around my room,*

   c. *a cramped space,*

   d. *the room of an only child,*

   e. *tidy,*

   f. *organized completely,*

   g. *with the possessory feel*

   h. *of everything*

   i. *in place,*

   j. *unmolested by any of the brothers and sisters I had for years longed to have and now, in my desolation, longed for with a special ache.*